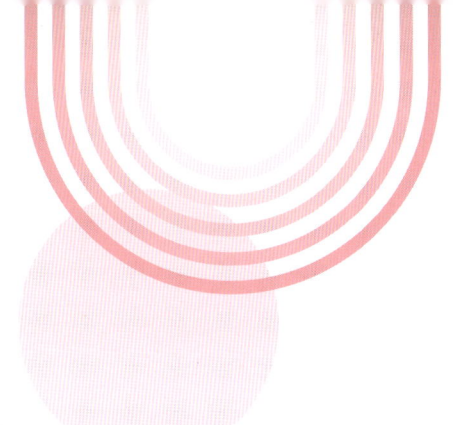

# Light & Breezy Knitwear

**15 Modern Patterns for Tanks, Tees, Skirts & Other Warm-Weather Garments**

### JOAN HO
**Founder of Knitwear by Joan,
Author of *Cable Knit Style*** 

PAGE STREET
PUBLISHING CO.

Copyright © 2025 Joan Ho

First published in 2025 by
Page Street Publishing Co.
27 Congress Street, Suite 1511
Salem, MA 01970
www.pagestreetpublishing.com

All rights reserved. No part of this book may be reproduced or used, in any form or by any means, electronic or mechanical, without prior permission in writing from the publisher.

Distributed by Macmillan, sales in Canada by The Canadian Manda Group.

29  28  27  26  25    1  2  3  4  5

ISBN-13: 979-8-89003-198-3

Library of Congress Control Number: 2024933597

Edited by Sarah Monroe
Cover and book design by Vienna Gambol for Page Street Publishing Co.
Photography by Joan Ho

Printed and bound in China

 Page Street Publishing protects our planet by donating to nonprofits like The Trustees, which focuses on local land conservation.

# Contents

*Introduction* — 6
*Before You Begin* — 9

## Feminine & Flirty — 19
### Lightweight Knits with Elegant & Delicate Details

Sakura Top — 21
Sakura Skirt — 29
Petunia Top — 35

## Knit + Athleisure = Knitleisure — 43
### Knits for Lounging & Staying Active

Iris Racerback Tank — 45
Poppy Pocket Tee — 53
Poppy Pocket Shorts — 65
Wisteria Tank — 75

## Festival & Beach Knits — 83
### Garments to Wear Under the Sun or in the Sand

Dahlia Bralette — 85
Ivy Mesh Bralette — 91
Ivy Mesh Skirt — 97
Mariposa Top — 107
Hollyberry Tee — 113

## Knits for Any Occasion — 119
### Versatile Tops to Dress Up or Down

Plume Halter — 121
Hibiscus Top — 127
Camellia Wrap Top — 135

*Techniques* — 142
*Resources* — 154
*Acknowledgments* — 155
*About the Author* — 156
*Index* — 157

# Introduction

Like many knitters, I will always appreciate a comfy sweater. However, in recent years I have found myself gravitating towards garments of the lightweight variety. While many may associate knitwear with the autumn chill or winter snow, that is a narrow interpretation of our craft. After all, knitters don't all live in climates that warrant thick and cozy sweaters. Having been born in Hong Kong, China, where temperatures are hot and humid almost year-round, the idea of warm weather knitwear has always felt natural to me. Winter knitwear was a foreign concept for my family until they immigrated to Canada—my parents had actually never owned a knit sweater until they left Asia (gasp!).

From a design perspective, I saw so much untapped potential in my yarn stash. The plethora of yarn that I've accumulated throughout the years became the basis of my inspiration for this collection. For me, it's always been about the yarn first and foremost. Fiber is the paint in my metaphorical palette and the foundation on which all my designs are based.

It wasn't much of a surprise to my family and friends when I announced that I had begun writing a second book even before my first book, *Cable Knit Style*, hit the bookshelves. While my journey as a first-time author was not without its challenges, it was rewarding in ways I had never experienced in my time as an independent knitwear designer. Being able to bring an idea from conception and nurture it into fruition was truly a magical experience for me. As someone who has always had a deep appreciation for physical media, having my designs published as a book was beyond my wildest dreams.

When brainstorming ideas for this sophomore book, the concept of a summer pattern book was always at the top of the list. I was beyond excited to play around with a new assortment of fibers and textures that I normally don't use for winter projects. Shimmery silks, luscious cottons and soft-to-the-touch bamboo fibers are just some of the yarns I'm drawn to for warm weather projects. While plant-based fibers can certainly be used year-round, the breathable, comfortable and luxurious fabrics they create are the perfect complement against bare, sun-kissed skin. It brought me so much joy rummaging through my stash, making swatches and seeing whether they matched the silhouettes I had envisioned. Some ideas worked out to great success on the first try, some required tweaking and some just outright failed.

I love the versatility of lightweight garment design, be it a knit bralette or a tank top. When working with finer fibers, you can be creative and experiment with density and textures just by combining different yarns together. It is so interesting to see how simply changing your needle size or adding another strand of yarn can impact how a garment drapes and sits on your body.

I'd also be remiss if I did not mention how *quickly* summer garments knit up. Lightweight knits typically need far less yarn, so that is a huge plus! With the exception of the Poppy Pocket Tee (page 53), all of the designs in this book are sleeveless, so you can cross off "sleeve island" as an excuse to not finish a project!

I love the saying that fashion is the ultimate form of self-expression, and as such, the beauty of this craft is that two individuals can wear the same article of clothing and can convey entirely different styles. Like my previous book and with all my independent designs, the patterns in this book are all size-inclusive, ranging from XS to 6XL. It is important to me that anyone who wants to knit my designs can do so and feel confident about how it fits on their body.

Whether you're planning to traverse the Arizona desert, stroll through the beaches of Rio de Janeiro or simply to survive the Melbourne heat, *Light & Breezy Knitwear* has a pattern for the occasion.

As always, the most rewarding part of my day is seeing my designs lovingly made, worn and cherished by other members of the handmade community. There's nothing I love more than to see photos, stories and reels of your works in progress as well as your finished projects! Please share them and tag #SummerKnitStyle and @knitwearbyjoan. I'm so excited to see what you come up with.

Happy making!

# Before You Begin

## PATTERN DIFFICULTY LEVELS

While some knitting experience is recommended, it is not required for all the projects in this book. Since the entire pattern book consists of garments, most projects will require shaping and finishing techniques such as seaming in order to ensure the best fit for your body. The patterns range from Beginner to Advanced level, with the majority of the projects designated under Beginner and Intermediate levels. The pattern difficulty level is dependent on, but is not limited to, the stitch pattern, construction method and other design elements used. I recommend reviewing the techniques used in each pattern (listed in the beginning of each pattern) to see if a particular project is a good fit for your skillset.

**Beginner:** Patterns classified as Advanced Beginner are a suitable choice for those newer to garment making. Both the Dahlia Bralette (page 85) and the Mariposa Top (page 107) are designated as Beginner patterns since both projects are knit flat, consist of simpler stitchwork and have minimal shaping. The smaller sizes of the projects also make them relatively quick projects to knit up.

**Intermediate:** Most patterns in this book fall under this level designation. These patterns typically involve more advanced techniques such as picking up stitches, armhole and/or waist shaping and finishing neckline/armhole edges.

**Advanced:** This level designation is a suitable choice if you are experienced in garment making and are comfortable with incorporating more advanced finishing techniques into your projects. Special notions such as snap-on buttons for the Poppy Pocket Tee (page 53) and Poppy Pocket Shorts (page 65) and elastic for the Sakura Top (page 21) involve manual installation and/or hand sewing.

## EASE & SELECTING YOUR SIZE

Every pattern in this book will include a schematic along with a sizing table. A schematic is a visual rendering of a design that provides an overview of the size and shape of the piece. The schematic provides a point of reference for determining the fit of a garment. The patterns in this book are designed and graded according to the Craft Yarn Council (CYC) Standard Body Measurements.

The sizing table provides specific measurements of the *finished garment* and will typically include the following measurements, listed in both metric and imperial equivalents.

**Body Circumference:** Measured at the widest point of the garment, typically at the bust. Please note that the full bust measurement is not the same number as your bra size. While your bra band is equivalent to your underbust measurement, the full bust is the largest part of your chest. However, you can select another size depending on your preference for ease.

**Garment Length:** The length of the garment from the bottom (usually the hem) to the top of the shoulders.

**Armhole Depth:** The vertical measurement of the underarm opening to the shoulder seams.

**Sleeve Circumference (if applicable):** Measured at the top of the sleeve. This is typically the widest point of the sleeve and corresponds with the upper bicep measurement.

**Sleeve Length (if applicable):** The length of the sleeve from the underarm to the cuffs.

## Understanding Ease

Ease is the way a garment fits on your body. In reference to knitwear design, there are three types of ease: Positive ease, neutral (or zero) ease, and negative ease. The patterns in this book will recommend the type and amount of ease to guide you in selecting the correct size. These recommendations are based on the chest circumference of both the finished garment and the wearer. For example, if your full bust is 34 inches (86 cm) and the pattern recommends 2 to 4 inches (5 to 10 cm) of positive ease, you should select the size that falls under the range of 36 to 38 inches (91 to 97 cm).

**Positive Ease:** This means that the finished measurements of a garment are larger than the measurements of the person wearing it. The additional fabric allows the wearer to move more comfortably and freely. A classic fit has several inches of ease, while some designs suggest significantly more ease for a relaxed fit. The Poppy Pocket Tee (page 53) is intended to be worn with a generous amount of ease.

**Neutral Ease:** This means that the finished measurements of a garment are equal to the measurements of the person wearing it. This type of fit results in a form-fitting garment. The Mariposa Top (page 107) is intended to be worn with neutral ease.

**Negative Ease:** This means the finished measurements of a garment are smaller than the measurements of the person wearing it. This fit allows for the knit fabric to stretch and hug your shape when you put it on. Most patterns with rib stitches are intended to be worn with negative ease since the resulting fabric will have a lot of stretch. The Plume Halter (page 121), Wisteria Tank (page 75) and Camellia Wrap Top (page 135) are all intended to be worn with negative ease.

# YARN & GAUGE

While specific yarns are recommended for all the projects in this book, you can also substitute for others. If you decide to use an alternate yarn, I recommend selecting a substitute yarn that is as close as possible to the original in thickness, weight and texture. That way, your finished garment will have a similar appearance, drape and wearability as the original pieces depicted in this book.

YarnSub (yarnsub.com) is an excellent resource to help you find yarn substitutes. All you have to do is type in the name of the yarn used in a pattern and the search results will return a list of substitute yarns based on gauge, texture and fiber content. Ravelry (ravelry.com/yarns) also provides a comprehensive directory of both current and discontinued yarns. I recommend calculating the amount of yarn you will need by the yards/meters rather than by weight. Always allocate enough yarn *in the same dye lot* to ensure there are no color variances and that your knit project will be the same color throughout.

## How to Knit a Gauge Swatch

A swatch is a piece of fabric, typically a square or rectangle in shape, that you knit prior to starting a pattern. The goal of swatching is to simulate the size and fit of your project as closely as possible to the original pattern. Although recommended knitting needle size(s) are provided for each pattern, every knitter has their own unique tension which will influence the swatch and therefore the size and fit of the finished garment. Each pattern in this book will provide the required stitch pattern(s) to swatch. Follow the steps below to successfully prepare for knitting your project.

**Knit a swatch in the specified pattern:** Knit a swatch that is large enough to represent the stitch pattern on the garment. All the patterns in this book call for a gauge within a 4-inch (10-cm) square. Therefore, it is recommended to knit at least a 5-inch (13-cm) square to account for any significant tension differences between your swatch and the one listed in the book.

The swatch pattern will specify whether it should be worked flat or in the round. Circular knitting can produce a different gauge than flat knitting due to a subtle variation in tension between knitting and purling. As such, it is important to knit your swatch as noted in the pattern for the best results.

**Block the swatch:** Block your swatch in the same manner you will use when finishing the final project. My preferred blocking method of choice is wet blocking, but your mileage may vary. You may notice the effects of blocking vary from yarn to yarn significantly.

**Measure the swatch:** Lay your swatch on a flat surface. Using a stitch gauge or simply a ruler, count and note the number of stitches within 4 inches (10 cm). Afterwards, count and note the number of rows/rounds within 4 inches (10 cm).

**Make adjustments if necessary:** Compare your gauge to the pattern and make adjustments if necessary. If you count more stitches per inch/centimeter on your swatch than is required for pattern gauge, you will need to swatch again with a larger needle. If no adjustments are made, your finished garment will be smaller than the measurements listed in the pattern.

If there are fewer stitches per inch/centimeter, you will need to swatch again using a smaller needle to achieve the correct gauge. If no adjustments are made, your finished garment will be larger than the measurements listed in the pattern.

If neither scenario occurs and your gauge matches, congratulations! You are ready to begin knitting your project.

## KNITTING CHARTS

A knitting chart is a visual representation of knitting stitches in a pattern. Charts are most commonly used for cable, lace or colorwork knitting. Rather than through text, symbols are used to denote a specific stitch pattern. Each cell represents one (1) stitch and each row of cells represents one (1) row or round.

Knitting charts are beneficial for multiple reasons. Charts help you visualize the design as a whole by allowing you to "preview" where the twists and turns will occur in the pattern. Knitting charts are also more efficient because there is only one set of instructions for both flat and circular knitting.

### How Do You Read a Knitting Chart?

All charts are read from the bottom up. The numbers on the left and/or right side of the chart represent that row or round. Once you have reached the top of the chart, you will start over from the beginning (row/round 1).

Every chart has a legend that defines what each of the symbols means. Each pattern has an abbreviations table with further instructions on what these symbols represent.

When working flat, the chart is read from right to left on right side (RS) rows and left to right on wrong side (WS) rows.

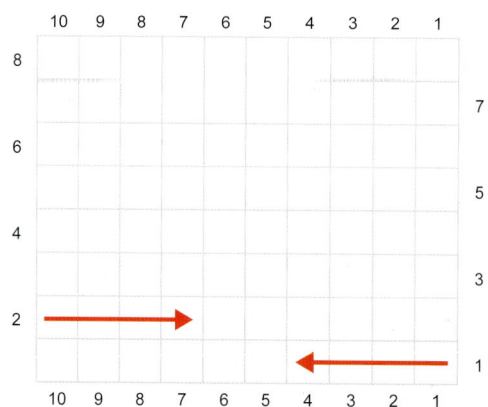

When working in the round, the cable chart is read from right to left on all rounds.

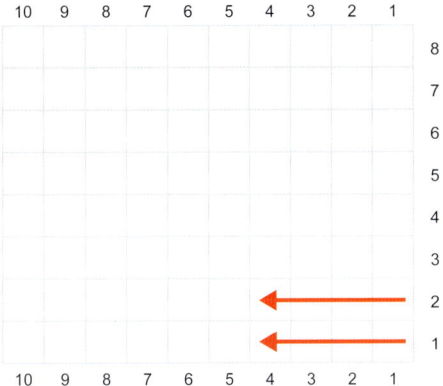

For simplicity, if a pattern calls for both knitting flat and knitting in the round, the knitting chart will have row numbering on both sides.

## NEEDLES & NOTIONS
### Recommended Needles

Each pattern will include a list of recommended needle sizes to use. As noted above, the needle sizes are suggestions only and will vary depending on your swatch. The needle size refers to the diameter of a needle, listed in both U.S. sizing and millimeters.

The pattern will also suggest the needle type and length to use for the project. Straight needles are used for flat knitting, in which the directions are to knit back and forth. Circular needles can be used for *both* flat knitting and knitting in the round. Due to the length of circular needles, they can accommodate projects with larger stitch counts. In addition, they also allow a knitter to work in a continuous round, such as for a hat or the body of a sweater. Since circular needles are more versatile and ergonomic to knit with, they are the most recommended needle type for the patterns in this book.

Where circular needles are listed, recommended lengths are also included. Although length is mostly a matter of preference, a general rule of thumb is to select a length that is several inches smaller than the circumference of your project. Avoid using a cord that is too long, otherwise the stitches of your project will be stretched out and so will the resulting fabric.

Double pointed needles, also referred to as DPNs, are needles with points on each end and are most often used for small circumference knitting such as hats, socks and sleeves. They are also commonly used in techniques that require the frequent slipping of stitches from one needle to the other, such as I-cord knitting.

## Notions

Notions are the additional materials or tools used in a project, ranging from necessities to accessories such as buttons or zippers.

*Elastic*

There are many types of elastic, including ones made specifically for swimwear, lingerie and athletic wear, among other applications. There are also thinner varieties such as shirring elastic, which are primarily used for machine sewing on non-knit fabrics. However, the elastic used in the patterns in this book are of the thicker variety since they need to hold the garment in place on your body. The Sakura Top (page 21) utilizes elastic to secure the top on your shoulders as well as at the waist, and the Sakura Skirt (page 29) has an elastic inserted at the waist to hold the skirt up. For these patterns, my preferred elastic of choice is the knit elastic as it is relatively soft and retains its shape well after wear. It is important to select an elastic at the recommended width, so it is neither too big or too small to fit inside the hem for that particular pattern. If an elastic is too small width-wise, you also run the risk of the elastic rolling and twisting inside the waistband. Lastly, be mindful that elastic also stretches with time, so the recommended length required for the pattern is usually smaller than the circumference of the garment.

*Sewing Needle & Thread*

There are several projects in this book that will require a sewing needle and matching thread, namely to sew the ends of an elastic band together to join it in the round. Ensure you select a sewing needle that is strong enough to pierce through the overlapping ends.

*Snap-On Buttons*

Snap-on buttons, also commonly called snap fasteners or press buttons, are round discs used to fasten clothing and serve the same purpose as traditional buttons. They are commonly used to fasten pockets, cardigan/jacket openings and attach hoods to coats, among other uses.

Snap-on buttons add a beautiful and professional finish to any knit garment. Unlike traditional buttons where it is necessary to knit buttonholes into the fabric, installing snap-buttons does not require preparation during the knitting process.

Installation is also relatively simple: You only need to accurately mark where both ends of the snap-button are to be placed and then attach them. There are many sizes of snap-on buttons available and the pattern will state the recommended size that is appropriate for the yarn weight used in the design.

*Stitch Holders*

A stitch holder is a tool that resembles an oversized safety pin and is used to temporarily hold live stitches to be returned to later. Stitch holders come in multiple sizes, and it is useful to have a variety on hand depending on the number of stitches you need to set aside for a particular project. When a stitch holder is not available, a spare knitting needle or scrap yarn can be used in its place.

*Stitch Markers*

Stitch markers are used to keep track of an important place in your project. **Standard stitch markers** are used to mark a point between one stitch and the next in the current row/round of your project. The most common placement of a stitch marker is to mark the beginning of the round of a project. A standard stitch marker is typically ring-shaped and does not close or open. As such, once it is placed it cannot be moved or removed until you reach where it is placed in your project. Once at the stitch marker, simply slip the stitch marker from the left needle to the right needle. Continue knitting as normal, until the pattern instructs you to remove the marker.

**Removable stitch markers** are any type of stitch markers that can either open and close or have a split ring structure where it has a beginning and an end. These stitch markers are used to mark a stitch itself or a point in the knit fabric. As such, removable stitch markers are more versatile as they can be added and removed from your project at any time, rather than having to wait until you knit to your desired spot. Note: Removable stitch markers can be used in place of standard stitch markers, but not the other way around.

If not specified, either type of stitch marker can be used. When a stitch marker is not available, a tied piece of yarn in a contrasting color can be used in its place.

*Tapestry Needle*

A tapestry needle, or darning needle, is a blunt tipped sewing needle used for weaving in loose ends. The needle typically has a large eye that makes threading yarn easy.

## HOW TO CARE FOR YOUR HANDKNITS

After spending hours working on your latest handknit, you are finally ready to bind off and wear your new garment with pride. Except, your work is not nearly done yet: Thoughtful aftercare of your knitwear is crucial to ensure your handmade pieces look beautiful for years to come. It will take time and effort, but the results will be well worth it. The last thing you want is premature pilling, shrinking or stretching, among other cursed verbs that do not belong in any knitter's vocabulary.

### Blocking

Blocking is the process of evening out stitches and setting your project to its finished dimensions using water or steam. Blocking is the final step in completing your project and should not be skipped, especially when it comes to garments. For either type of blocking, you will need a measuring tape (or ruler) and pins to set your work. You may use any flat surface to block your project, although many knitters like using tools such as blocking mats so you can move the piece from room to room if need be. A towel alone may be used in place of a mat in some circumstances but will not be as effective since it is trickier to secure your project to it.

### Wet Blocking

Soak your project in a gentle wool wash according to your yarn label instructions (see below on my best tips on how to wash your project). Alternatively, rather than submerging your entire project in water, you can use a spray bottle to dampen the project just enough that it can easily be shaped. Once as much of the water has been removed from your project as possible, lay your damp project right side up on your blocking surface. Gently position your work so that there are no folds or wrinkles in the fabric. Using the sizing chart of your pattern as a guide, insert your pins at an angle through your fabric and into your blocking surface to set your project to the finished dimensions. Allow the project to air dry before removing the pins. For larger projects, this can take up to a week.

### Steam Blocking

When it comes to steam blocking, there is more flexibility in the order of the steps. You can set your project with pins first and then apply steam, or apply steam to your project first and then set your project with pins. To apply steam, set your steamer to the lowest setting (you can adjust this afterwards) and hover your steamer over your project at a distance. Alternatively, you can place a damp towel over your project and apply your iron directly to the towel. Like wet blocking, once the project is dry, you can remove your pins.

### Washing

Every fiber has its own specific aftercare instructions, so it is important to read the yarn label carefully for specific directions. Projects made with 100% synthetic fibers such as acrylic or polyester can be machine washed, although a delicate cycle is still preferred. For all other projects made with natural fibers or mixed blend fibers, handwashing will almost always be the recommended method. An exception is projects made with superwash wool, which is a yarn that has either been coated or chemically treated to allow for machine washing or handwashing at a wider range of temperatures. Regardless of superwash status, some knitters will still prefer to use the tried-and-true method of handwashing.

When your knit is ready to be washed, fill a small basin or tub with lukewarm water. You do not want to use water that is too cold or too hot, as extreme temperatures can "shock" the individual fibers and cause the fabric to felt. Gently place your project into the basin, ensuring it is fully submerged. At this point, add your wool wash (my favorite brand is Soak; they have a variety of fragrances as well as unscented). Some knitters like to use this time to massage the fabric, which helps with evening out stitches. This is especially useful if this is also the first time washing and blocking your project.

Soak your project according to the instructions on your wash label (typically 10 to 15 minutes) prior to rinsing. Some wool washes are also rinse-free, which saves water and eliminates one extra step. Once the suds are gone, take your knit out of the basin and squeeze out as much water as possible. Alternatively, what I like to do is pour the water out first and then use my palms to press out as much water as possible as a first step.

When handling your knit, it is important to avoid lifting your project from one end while it is still drenched. Doing so will cause the water to weigh down one side of your project and lead to stretching. Do not wring your project, as that can cause agitation in addition to wrinkling your fabric. Once you have squeezed out as much water as possible, lay your project on a towel to begin the drying process. For larger garments, you may want to use the towel to press out any excess water that you were unable to remove earlier. Otherwise, you can leave your project out to dry. I like to place a blocking mat underneath the towel, so I don't damage my floors.

### Storage

Proper storage is important to ensure the longevity of your knitwear. If possible, projects should be folded, stored flat and placed in a container or in a dresser away from direct sunlight. Most garments should not be hung on clothes hangers, as the weight of the garment will strain the stitches and lead to stretching. Some hangers, with wooden ones being a nastier culprit, also have a tendency to stretch out and deform the shoulders of a garment. For lighter weight garments, some hangers such as curved or velvet ones will not have this issue; however, the safer bet is still to fold your knitwear.

Furthermore, proper storage of your knits can prevent a moth infestation in your knitwear. In many climates, moths can be a big problem because they eat away at natural fibers. Lavender sachets are commonly placed in wardrobes and used to repel moths and can be purchased at a low price from your local farmer's market or supermarket.

Before You Begin

# Feminine & Flirty

## Lightweight Knits with Elegant & Delicate Details

I am a strong believer that effective knitwear design has the ability to invoke feelings of confidence and pride in both maker and wearer. For this book, I wanted to create a set of patterns to feel sexy and confident in. These designs are unapologetically feminine with form-fitting details that accentuate, rather than hide, a body's natural curvatures.

One of the reasons I love designing with lighter weight yarns is the versatility that they bring to a project. With thinner yarns, you have more options to play with tension. Instead of knitting at the manufacturer's recommended gauge, you can create a more relaxed fabric by working with larger needles. You can also do the opposite by using smaller needles, holding your yarn double or both. I had a lot of fun doing just that when designing the Petunia Top (page 35). Larger needles were used to construct the drape and delicate nature of the ruffle, while the bra cups required a tighter gauge for density and support. At even a fraction of a different gauge, the result would have been a stiffer or looser fabric that would have changed the design completely.

Lacework is another design element that comes to mind for flirty, feminine knits. The Sakura set, consisting of a top (page 21) and skirt (page 29), are beautiful when worn together but can also be styled separately for two wholly different looks.

# Sakura Top

The Sakura Top is a flirty and fun addition to any summer wardrobe. Adorned with a voluminous lace ruffle and worn off the shoulder, this cold shoulder top can be dressed up or down depending on the occasion. Cropped with an elastic at the waist, you can adjust the fit as you wish. Perfect for date night or an afternoon out in the park, you'll undoubtedly feel like the best version of yourself no matter what you wear it with. While designed to be paired with the Sakura Skirt (page 29), the Sakura Top would also make a cute outfit with a pair of shorts or a mini skirt. The ruffle is a labor of love, but worth every stitch.

## Construction Notes

The top is worked in the round from the top down, beginning with a folded hem and lace ruffle. The ruffle is bound off using the I-cord bind off method for a clean finished edge. Stitches are then picked up on the underside of the folded hem for the body. Stitches are skipped on both sides to create the arm openings. The body is worked top down in the round with moderate decreases to create a tapered waist. The bottom of the top is finished with another folded hem. After blocking, elastics are inserted and secured into both of the folded hems. Note: The ruffle will appear very large before the insertion of the elastic.

## SKILL LEVEL

Intermediate

## SIZING

XS (S, M, L, XL) (2XL, 3XL, 4XL, 5XL, 6XL)

Bust circumference of 30 (34, 37.25, 41.25, 46) (50, 54, 57.25, 61.25, 66)" / 76 (86, 95, 105, 117) (127, 137, 146, 156, 168) cm, blocked

## Materials

### Yarn

DK weight, Pickles Booboo in 109 (100% bamboo), 109 yds (100 m) per 50-g skein

An alternate sample was also knit with Drops Belle in Silver.

Any DK weight yarn can be used for this pattern as long as it matches gauge.

## Yardage/Meterage

750 (905, 955, 1150, 1240) (1360, 1465, 1610, 1780, 1930) yds / 685 (825, 875, 1050, 1135) (1245, 1340, 1470, 1630, 1765) m of DK weight yarn

## Needles

**For hem:** US 4 (3.5 mm), 32- to 60-inch (80- to 150-cm) circular needle

**For ruffle and top:** US 6 (4 mm), 24- to 60-inch (60- to 150-cm) circular needle

## Notions

0.75" / 20-mm elastic (recommended length: 0.5 inch / 1 cm less than your shoulder circumference)

0.5" / 13-mm elastic (recommended length: 0.5 inch / 1 cm less than your waist circumference)

Removable stitch marker

Safety pin

Scissors

Scrap yarn in a contrasting color

Sewing needle and matching thread

Stitch markers

Tapestry needle

Feminine & Flirty

## GAUGE

24 sts x 32 rounds = 4 inches (10 cm) in stockinette st worked in the round using smaller needles (blocked)

20 sts x 24 rounds = 4 inches (10 cm) in stockinette st worked in the round using larger needles (blocked)

## TECHNIQUES

*Backwards Loop Cast On (page 142)*

*I-Cord Bind Off (page 148)*

*Whip Stitch (page 150)*

## ABBREVIATIONS

| | |
|---|---|
| BOR | beginning of round |
| CDD | centered double decrease: slip 2 sts together knitwise; knit 1 st; using the tip of your left needle, pick up the 2 sts you slipped and pass them over the knitted st and off of the needle [2 sts decreased] |
| dec | decrease |
| inc | increase |
| k | knit |
| k1tbl | knit through the back loop |
| k2tog | knit 2 sts together [1 st decreased] |
| p | purl |
| pm | place marker |
| rem | remain(ing) |
| rep | repeat |
| sm | slip marker |
| ssk | slip 2 sts knitwise, one at a time; move both stitches back to the left needle; knit these 2 sts together through the back loops [1 st decreased] |
| st(s) | stitch(es) |
| stm(s) | stitch marker(s) |
| WS | wrong side |
| yo | yarnover |

# SIZING CHART

| | XS | S | M | L | XL | 2XL | 3XL | 4XL | 5XL | 6XL | |
|---|---|---|---|---|---|---|---|---|---|---|---|
| A) Body Circumference | 30 | 34 | 37.25 | 41.25 | 46 | 50 | 54 | 57.25 | 61.25 | 66 | in |
| | 76 | 86 | 95 | 105 | 117 | 127 | 137 | 146 | 156 | 168 | cm |
| B) Waist Circumference | 27.25 | 30 | 32.75 | 36.75 | 40.75 | 44.75 | 48.75 | 50.75 | 53.25 | 57.25 | in |
| | 69 | 76 | 83 | 93 | 103 | 113 | 124 | 129 | 135 | 146 | cm |
| C) Shoulder Circumference (before adding elastic) | 39.5 | 44.5 | 49.25 | 54 | 60 | 66 | 70.75 | 75.5 | 80.5 | 86.5 | in |
| | 101 | 113 | 125 | 137 | 153 | 168 | 180 | 192 | 204 | 220 | cm |
| D) Ruffle Circumference | 79.25 | 88.75 | 98.5 | 108 | 120 | 132 | 141.5 | 151.25 | 160.75 | 172.75 | in |
| | 201 | 226 | 250 | 274 | 305 | 335 | 360 | 384 | 409 | 439 | cm |
| E) Garment Length (measured from underarm) | 9.25 | 10.5 | 10.75 | 10.75 | 10.75 | 10.75 | 10.75 | 11.5 | 12.75 | 13 | in |
| | 24 | 27 | 28 | 28 | 28 | 28 | 28 | 30 | 33 | 34 | cm |

The top is designed with 0 to 2 inches (0 to 5 cm) of neutral to positive ease. Sample shown is knit in size XS.

# SCHEMATIC

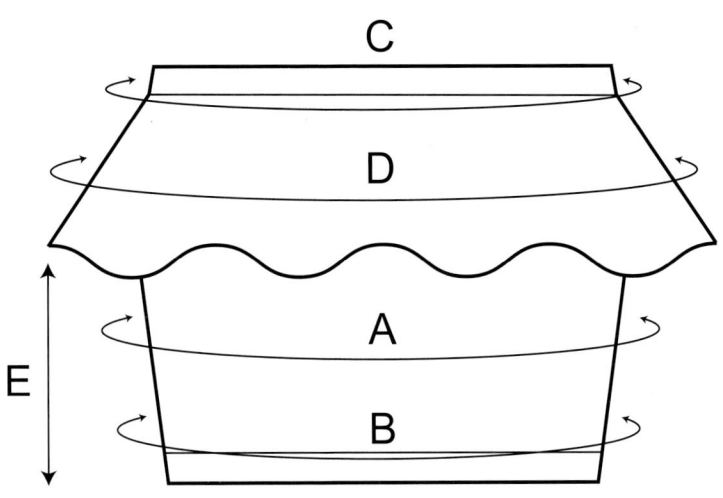

Feminine & Flirty

# SAKURA TOP PATTERN

## TOP HEM

Using US 4 (3.5 mm) needles, cast on 198 (222, 246, 270, 300) (330, 354, 378, 402, 432) sts using the longtail cast on method, leaving a 4-inch (10-cm) tail to close the gap in the folded hem later. Pm and join for knitting in the round.

**Rounds 1–6:** K all sts.

**Round 7 (turning round):** P all sts.

**Round 8–14:** K all sts.

## Create Folded Hem

Fold your work so the purl round is now the bottom edge. Pick up the corresponding st from the cast on edge and place on left needle. K it together with the st from the current round. Repeat until you reach 4 sts before the BOR marker, k4 from the current round. This will leave a small opening for you to insert elastic afterwards. Place a removable stm at the first stitch of the round.

Switch to US 6 (4 mm) needles for the ruffle.

**Next round (inc):** *K1, yo; rep from * until end. [396 (444, 492, 540, 600) (660, 708, 756, 804, 864) sts]

K 1 round.

**Rounds 1–48:** Work Chart A (page 27) a total of 2 times. [33 (37, 41, 45, 50) (55, 59, 63, 67, 72) chart repeats per round]

> **TIP:** Use stms between each or several lace repeat(s) to keep track of the pattern repeats. The ruffle will look extremely large at this point—this is normal.

## I-Cord Bind Off

> **NOTE:** *I-cord bind offs can be tight, so feel free to use a larger size needle or be mindful and bind off more loosely.*

Using your right needle, insert it between the first and second stitch of your left needle. Wrap working yarn around your right needle and draw it up so you have a new stitch. Place the new stitch onto the left needle. Repeat one more time so you have a total of 2 new sts.

**Next step:** K1, ssk from the left needle. Move the 2 sts back to the left needle.

Repeat last step until no hem sts rem. Bind off and seam the ends of the I-cord together.

Leave a tail long enough to weave in any ends, so there are no gaps from the beginning and end of the I-cord bind off.

## BODY

Position your work so the WS of the ruffle is facing you and the purl round of the folded hem (round 7 of the hem) is at the top. You will now be picking up sts from the bottom of the folded hem (where you seamed it shut) and working from the top down to create the rest of the top.

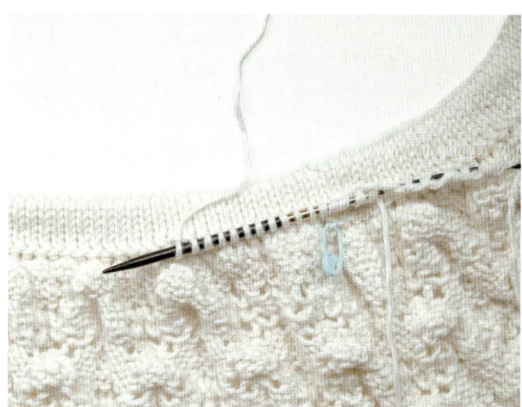

*Light & Breezy Knitwear*

Using US 4 (3.5 mm) and the backwards loop method for all cast on sts, begin at the removable stm and pick up and k68 (78, 86, 94, 104) (116, 124, 132, 138, 150), loosely cast on 11 (12, 13, 15, 17) (17, 19, 20, 23, 24) sts, pm for side, loosely cast on 11 (12, 13, 15, 17) (17, 19, 20, 23, 24) sts, skip the next 31 (33, 37, 41, 46) (49, 53, 57, 63, 66) sts from the folded hem edge, pick and k68 (78, 86, 94, 104) (116, 124, 132, 138, 150), loosely cast on 11 (12, 13, 15, 17) (17, 19, 20, 23, 24) sts, pm for new BOR, loosely cast on 11 (12, 13, 15, 17) (17, 19, 20, 23, 24) sts. **Note:** The last 31 (33, 37, 41, 46) (49, 53, 57, 63, 66) sts from the folded hem edge will also be skipped. Remove the removable stm. [180 (204, 224, 248, 276) (300, 324, 344, 368, 396) sts]

**Next round:** K32 (37, 42, 45, 50) (54, 59, 63, 69, 72), pm, (k1, p1) 13 (14, 14, 17, 19) (21, 22, 23, 23, 27) times, pm, k32 (37, 42, 45, 50) (54, 59, 63, 69, 72), sm, k until end.

**Next round:** K until stm, sm, (k1, p1) until stm, sm, k until side stm, sm, k until end.

Repeat last round until piece measures 6 (6, 5.5, 5.5, 5) (5, 5, 4.5, 4.5, 4)" / 15 (15, 14, 14, 13) (13, 13, 11, 11, 10) cm from the pick up edge.

## Begin Waist Decreases (Optional)

If you prefer a more relaxed fit and would like to skip the shaping, continue repeating the last round until piece measures 8.5 (9.75, 9.75, 9.75, 10) (10, 10, 10.75, 12, 12.25)" / 22 (25, 25, 25, 25) (25, 25, 27, 30, 31) cm, or until desired length from the pick up edge. You can also adjust the number of decrease repeats to your preference. Proceed to the "Create Folded Hem" section.

**Round 1 (dec):** K4, ssk, k until stm, sm, (k1, p1) until stm, sm, k until 6 sts before side stm, k2tog, k4, sm, k4, ssk, k until 6 sts before BOR stm, k2tog, k4. [176 (200, 220, 244, 272) (296, 320, 340, 364, 392) sts rem, 4 sts decreased]

**Rounds 2–5:** K until stm, sm, (k1, p1) until stm, sm, k until side stm, sm, k until end.

Repeat rounds 1–5 a total of 3 (5, 6, 6, 7) (7, 7, 9, 11, 12) more times until 164 (180, 196, 220, 244) (268, 292, 304, 320, 344) sts rem.

### Create Folded Hem

**Next round:** K all sts, removing all markers except for the BOR stm. Using a tapestry needle, insert a lifeline in the round you just knit.

**Next 4 rounds:** K all sts.

**Next round (turning round):** P all sts.

**Next 4 rounds:** K all sts.

Bind off and leave a tail approximately 3x the circumference of the body. Fold the hem inwards and use the tail to whip stitch the bind off edge to the round indicated by the lifeline. Leave an approximately 1-inch (3-cm) gap for inserting the elastic later. Remove lifeline.

## FINISHING

Block your project using your preferred method.

Measure a piece of 0.75" (20-mm) elastic to your preferred length for the shoulder elastic (recommended length is 0.5 inch / 1 cm less than your shoulder circumference). Keep in mind elastic bands become looser with time.

Use a safety pin to insert and guide the elastic through the folded hem. When the ends of your elastic meet, use your sewing needle and thread to sew the ends together securely. Use the whip stitch technique with the tail from your cast on to close the final gap to enclose your elastic into the folded hem. Tie off and weave in any loose ends.

Measure a piece of 0.5" (13-mm) elastic to your preferred length for the waist elastic (recommended length is 0.5 inch / 1 cm less than your waist circumference). Use the same technique as in the previous paragraph to insert and sew the elastic in place.

# CHART A

When working in the round, the chart is read from right to left on all rounds.

**NOTE:** *For all sizes, the chart will need to be worked twice to achieve 48 rounds.*

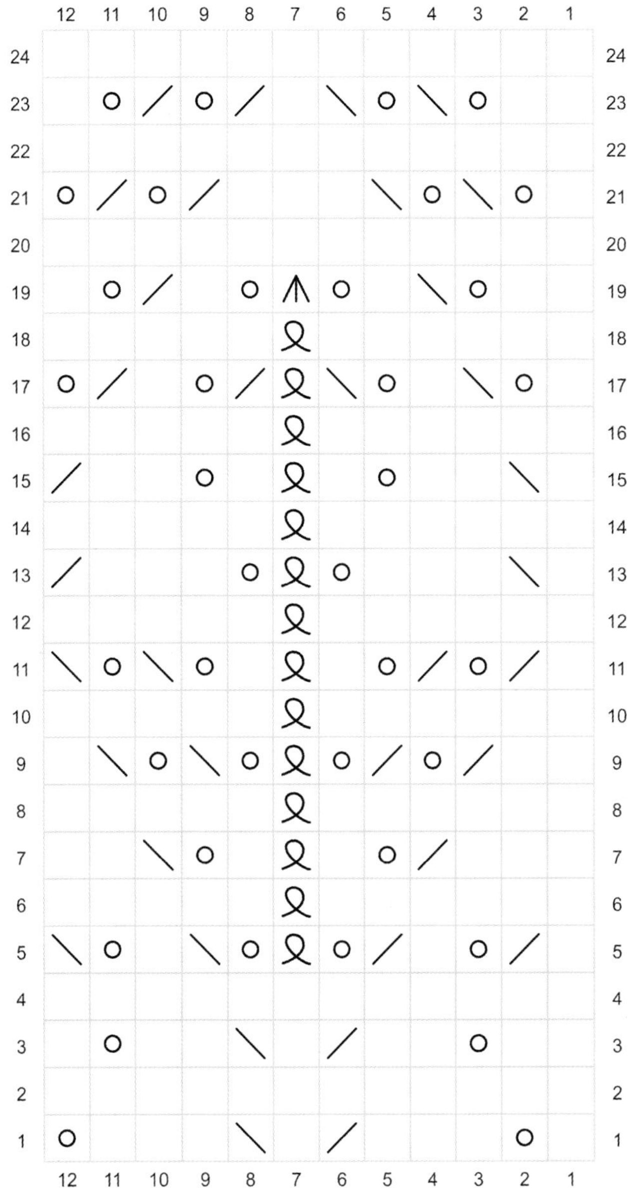

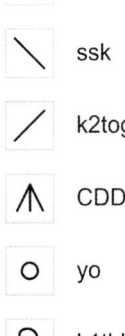

| Symbol | Meaning |
|---|---|
| (blank) | k |
| \ | ssk |
| / | k2tog |
| ∧ | CDD |
| O | yo |
| Ω | k1tbl |

# Sakura Skirt

If you're looking for a maxi skirt that is the perfect combination of simplicity and elegance, look no further than the Sakura Skirt. This slip-on skirt has a narrow A-line silhouette with an elastic, allowing it to sit at your natural waist with ease and comfort. Knit with a cotton yarn to create a soft and stretchy garment, the skirt is made to sculpt your shape and flatter your curves. Combining the simplicity of stockinette stitch with lace details, the result is a stunning accompaniment to the Sakura Top (page 21). If not worn as a set, the pattern is also subtle enough that it can also be easily paired with other tops and layering pieces.

## Construction Notes

*The skirt is worked in the round from the top down, beginning with a folded hem. The entire skirt is knit in the round beginning with stockinette stitch. Gradual increases are incorporated into the piece to accommodate for the hips. Once all the increases are completed, the lace pattern begins. The lace chart is worked a total of three times, with a section of stockinette stitch alternating in between. Finally, the skirt is bound off using the I-cord bind off method and elastic is inserted into the folded hem.*

> **NOTE:** *The sizing table lists the length of the skirt before and after the lace pattern. Feel free to adjust according to your preferred length.*

## SKILL LEVEL
Intermediate

## SIZING
XS (S, M, L, XL) (2XL, 3XL, 4XL, 5XL, 6XL)

Waist circumference of 25.25 (27.5, 30, 34.75, 38.5) (42, 46.75, 48, 51.5, 54)" / 64 (70, 76, 88, 98) (107, 119, 122, 131, 137) cm, blocked. This measurement is prior to the insertion of the elastic.

## Materials

### Yarn
DK weight, Drops Belle in Silver (53% cotton, 33% rayon, 14% linen/flax), 131 yds (120 m) per 50-g skein

Any DK weight yarn can be used for this pattern as long as it matches gauge.

### Yardage/Meterage
1270 (1465, 1610, 1900, 2120) (2350, 2650, 2760, 3010, 3180) yds / 1160 (1340, 1470, 1735, 1940) (2150, 2425, 2525, 2750, 2910) m of DK weight yarn

### Needles
**For waistband:** *US 4 (3.5 mm), 16- to 47-inch (40- to 120-cm) circular needle*

**For skirt:** *US 6 (4 mm), 32- to 60-inch (80- to 150-cm) circular needle*

### Notions
*0.75" / 20-mm elastic (recommended length: 0.5 inch / 1 cm less than your waist)*

*Removable stitch markers*

*Safety pin*

*Scissors*

*Sewing needle and matching thread*

*Stitch markers*

*Tapestry needle*

## GAUGE

20 sts x 24 rounds = 4 inches (10 cm) in stockinette st worked in the round using larger needles (blocked)

## TECHNIQUES

I-Cord Bind Off (page 148)

Whip Stitch (page 150)

# ABBREVIATIONS

| | |
|---|---|
| BOR | beginning of round |
| CDD | centered double decrease: slip 2 sts together knitwise; knit 1 st; using the tip of your left needle, pick up the 2 sts you slipped and pass them over the knitted st and off of the needle [2 sts decreased] |
| inc | increase |
| k | knit |
| k1tbl | knit through the back loop |
| k2tog | knit 2 sts together [1 st decreased] |
| m1b | make 1 below: insert right needle into the st below the next st, k1 [1 st increased] |
| p | purl |
| pm | place marker |
| rem | remain(ing) |
| rep | repeat |
| ssk | slip 2 sts knitwise, one at a time; move both stitches back to the left needle; knit these 2 sts together through the back loops [1 st decreased] |
| st(s) | stitch(es) |
| sm(s) | stitch marker(s) |
| yo | yarnover |

# SIZING CHART

| | XS | S | M | L | XL | 2XL | 3XL | 4XL | 5XL | 6XL | |
|---|---|---|---|---|---|---|---|---|---|---|---|
| A) Waist Circumference | 25.25 | 27.5 | 30 | 34.75 | 38.5 | 42 | 46.75 | 48 | 51.5 | 54 | in |
| | 64 | 70 | 76 | 88 | 98 | 107 | 119 | 122 | 131 | 137 | cm |
| B) Skirt Length before Lace Pattern | 19 | 19.75 | 20.5 | 21.25 | 22 | 22.75 | 23.5 | 24.25 | 25 | 25.75 | in |
| | 48 | 50 | 52 | 54 | 56 | 58 | 60 | 62 | 64 | 65 | cm |
| C) Skirt Length | 36.25 | 37 | 37.75 | 38.5 | 39.25 | 40 | 40.75 | 41.5 | 42.25 | 43 | in |
| | 92 | 94 | 96 | 98 | 100 | 102 | 104 | 105 | 107 | 109 | cm |
| D) Skirt Circumference at Hip | 33.5 | 36.75 | 40 | 46.5 | 51.25 | 56 | 62.5 | 64 | 68.75 | 72 | in |
| | 85 | 93 | 102 | 118 | 130 | 142 | 159 | 163 | 175 | 183 | cm |
| E) Skirt Circumference at Bottom | 50.5 | 55.25 | 60 | 69.5 | 76.75 | 84 | 93.5 | 96 | 103.25 | 108 | in |
| | 128 | 140 | 152 | 177 | 195 | 213 | 237 | 244 | 262 | 274 | cm |

*The skirt is designed with 0 to 4 inches (0 to 10 cm) of neutral to positive ease at the hip. If in between sizes and/or there is a significant difference in your waist and hip measurements, select the size closest to your waist measurement. Sample shown is knit in size XS.*

# SCHEMATIC

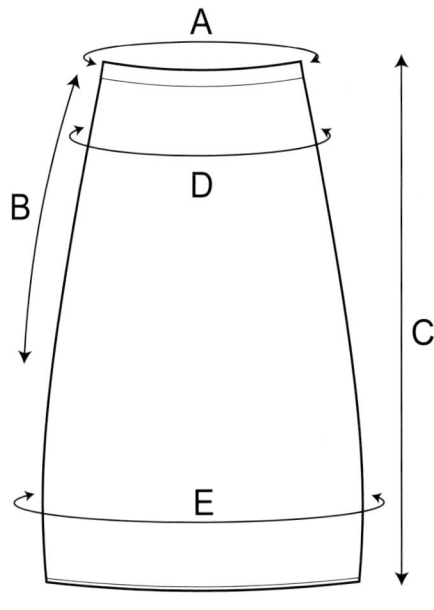

Feminine & Flirty

# SAKURA SKIRT PATTERN

## TOP HEM

Using US 4 (3.5 mm) needles, cast on 126 (138, 150, 174, 192) (210, 234, 240, 258, 270) sts using the longtail cast on method, leaving a 4-inch (10-cm) tail to close the gap in the folded hem later. Pm and join for knitting in the round.

**Rounds 1–7:** K all sts.

**Round 8:** P all sts.

**Round 9–16:** K all sts.

## Create Folded Hem

Fold your work so the purl round is now the bottom edge. Pick up the corresponding st from the cast on edge and place on left needle. K it together with the st from the current round. Repeat until you reach 4 sts before the BOR marker, k4 from the current round. This will leave a small opening for you to insert elastic afterwards.

Switch to US 6 (4 mm) needles.

**Next round (inc):** *M1b, k3; rep from * until end. Place a removable stm at the first stitch. [168 (184, 200, 232, 256) (280, 312, 320, 344, 360) sts]

K all rounds for 6 (6.25, 6.5, 6.75, 7) (7.25, 7.5, 7.75, 8, 8.25)" / 15 (16, 17, 17, 18) (18, 19, 20, 20, 21) cm, measured from the removable stm placed in the previous increase round. Switch to longer circular needles when necessary.

**Next round (inc):** *M1b, k4; rep from * until end. Place a removable stm at the first stitch. [210 (230, 250, 290, 320) (350, 390, 400, 430, 450) sts]

K all rounds for 6 (6.25, 6.5, 6.75, 7) (7.25, 7.5, 7.75, 8, 8.25)" / 15 (16, 17, 17, 18) (18, 19, 20, 20, 21) cm, measured from the removable stm placed in the previous increase round.

**Next round (inc):** *M1b, k5; rep from * until end. Place a removable stm at the first stitch. [252 (276, 300, 348, 384) (420, 468, 480, 516, 540) sts]

K all rounds for 6 (6.25, 6.5, 6.75, 7) (7.25, 7.5, 7.75, 8, 8.25)" / 15 (16, 17, 17, 18) (18, 19, 20, 20, 21) cm, measured from the removable stm placed in the previous increase round.

**Important:** *Note the skirt length in the sizing chart before proceeding with the lace pattern. From here on out, you will be adding 17.5 inches (44 cm) in length to the skirt. If you wish to lengthen the skirt, k additional rounds of stockinette here. You may also wish to add additional lace and stockinette repeats instead. Each additional repeat will add 7.25 inches (18 cm) in length. If you are adding length, you will also require more yarn than the estimate provides. Additional length may also add more weight to the skirt and cause it to stretch.*

## Begin Lace Pattern

**\*Rounds 1–24:** Work Chart A. [21 (23, 25, 29, 32) (35, 39, 40, 43, 45) chart repeats per round]

**Rounds 25–48:** K all sts.\*\*

**TIP:** *I recommend placing stms between the lace chart repeats to better manage your work and removing them once the last round of the lace chart is complete.*

Repeat from * to ** 1 more time.

Repeat rounds 1–24 of Chart A.

K all sts for 2 rounds.

## I-Cord Bind Off

Using your right needle, insert it between the first and second stitch of your left needle. Wrap working yarn around your right needle and draw it up so you have a new stitch. Place the new stitch onto the left needle. Repeat one more time so you have a total of 2 new sts.

**Next step:** K1, ssk from the left needle. Move the 2 sts back to the left needle.

Repeat the last step until no hem sts rem. Bind off and seam the ends of the I-cord together.

Leave a tail long enough to weave in any ends, so there are no gaps from the beginning and end of the I-cord bind off.

## FINISHING

Block your project using your preferred method.

Measure a piece of elastic to your preferred length (recommended length is 0.5 inch / 1 cm smaller than your waist). Keep in mind elastic bands become looser with time.

Use a safety pin to insert and guide the elastic through the folded hem. When the ends of your elastic meet, use your sewing needle and thread to sew the ends together securely. Use the whip stitch technique with the tail from your cast on to close the final gap to enclose your elastic into the folded hem. Tie off and weave in any loose ends.

# CHART A

When working in the round, the chart is read from right to left on all rounds.

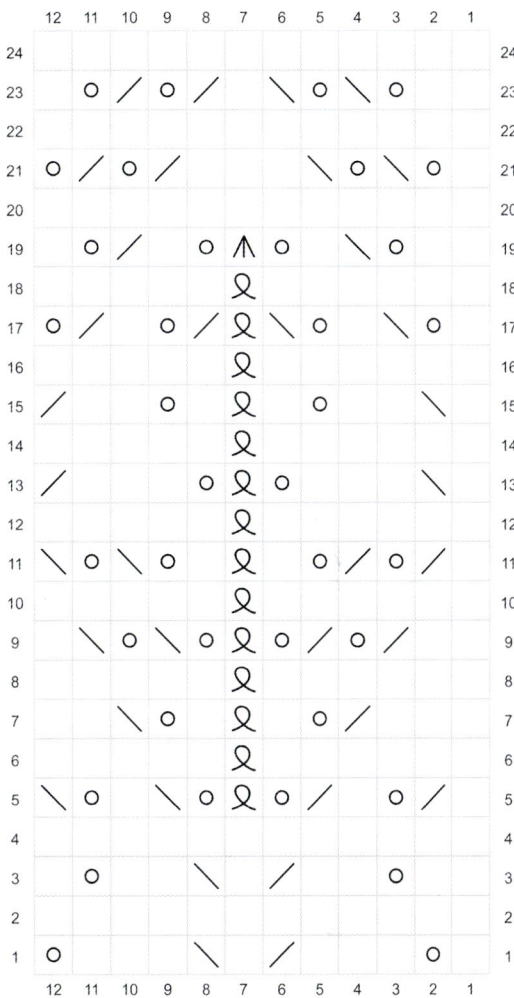

# Petunia Top

The Petunia Top is the definition of whimsical feminine energy. The airy fabric, plunging V-neckline and ruffled body are details that, while lovely on their own, create that coveted "wow" factor for any outfit when brought together. Not to mention, the stockinette stitch fabric also provides the perfect canvas to show off that special hand-dyed yarn in your stash.

Knit with fingering weight yarn, this design uses tension in a variety of ways that creates both density and delicateness wherever needed. Holding two strands together at the bust creates a firmer fabric at the chest for additional support, while using a single strand with larger needles results in a lightweight and drapey ruffle.

There is no shortage of outfit options. Pair it with leather pants and a clutch for a sexy date night ensemble, or dress it down with jeans for a shopping trip with the girls. The front ties also allow you to adjust to your preferred fit and level of modesty depending on the occasion.

## Construction Notes

*The top is worked both in the round as well as flat. You will begin by working the bra cups separately from the bottom up, and later completing the ruffle from the top down.*

*You will begin with the base of each triangular bra cup, working flat. Decreases will be worked on each side of the cup until you reach the top, after which the remaining sts will be worked in an I-cord to create the strap. After both cups are completed, you will be casting on the back stitches and creating the folded underbust hem where the I-cord tie will be inserted later. These sts will be worked flat, leaving an opening between the two cups so the top can be adjusted with ties.*

*After the underbust hem is completed, stitches will be picked up around the hem and the ruffle will be joined and worked in the round from the top down. Finally, an I-cord tie is worked and inserted into the underbust hem.*

## SKILL LEVEL
*Advanced Beginner*

## SIZING
XS (S, M, L, XL) (2XL, 3XL, 4XL, 5XL, 6XL)

Underbust circumference of 28.25 (32.25, 36.25, 40.25, 44.25) (48.25, 52.25, 56.25, 60.25, 64.25)" / 73 (83, 93, 103, 113) (123, 134, 144, 154, 164) cm, blocked

## Materials

### Yarn
Fingering weight, Summer Camp Fibers Yarn Goosebumps in Cotton Candy (90% superwash merino, 10% nylon), 246 yds (225 m) per 100-g skein

Any fingering weight yarn can be used for this pattern as long as it matches gauge.

### Yardage/Meterage
350 (430, 485, 555, 615) (685, 745, 815, 875, 945) yds / 325 (395, 445, 510, 565) (630, 685, 750, 805, 870) m of fingering weight yarn

### Needles
**For cups and underbust hem:** US 5 (3.75 mm), 24- to 60-inch (60- to 150-cm) circular needles

**For ruffle:** US 7 (4.5 mm) circular needles*

**For I-cord:** US 4 (3.5 mm) double pointed needles

*Any length smaller than the ruffle circumference will work, but minimum of 36-inch (90-cm) cord length is recommended due to the large number of sts.

(Materials continued)

## Notions
Removable stitch marker
Safety pin
Stitch marker
Tapestry needle

## GAUGE
22 sts x 27 rounds = 4 inches (10 cm) in stockinette stitch with US 5 (3.75 mm) needles and yarn held double (blocked)

## TECHNIQUES
Backwards Loop Cast On (page 142)
Horizontal Invisible Seam (page 149)
I-Cord (page 153)

# ABBREVIATIONS

| | |
|---|---|
| 0 or - | no stitch / step does not apply to your size |
| DPN(s) | double pointed needles |
| k | knit |
| k2tog | knit 2 sts together [1 st decreased] |
| m1l | make 1 left: use the left needle to pick up the strand between the last worked st and the next unworked st from front to back, knit this st through the back loop [1 st increased] |
| p | purl |
| pm | place marker |
| rem | remain(ing) |
| rep | repeat |
| RS | right side |
| ssk | slip 2 sts knitwise, one at a time; move both stitches back to the left needle; knit these 2 sts together through the back loops [1 st decreased] |
| st(s) | stitch(es) |
| WS | wrong side |

Light & Breezy Knitwear

# SIZING CHART

|  | XS | S | M | L | XL | 2XL | 3XL | 4XL | 5XL | 6XL |  |
|---|---|---|---|---|---|---|---|---|---|---|---|
| A) Cup Width | 5.5 | 6.5 | 7.5 | 8.5 | 9.5 | 10.5 | 11.5 | 12.5 | 13.5 | 14.5 | in |
|  | 14 | 17 | 19 | 22 | 25 | 27 | 30 | 32 | 35 | 37 | cm |
| B) Cup Height | 5.5 | 6.5 | 7.75 | 8.75 | 10 | 11 | 12.25 | 13.25 | 14.25 | 15.5 | in |
|  | 14 | 17 | 20 | 23 | 26 | 28 | 31 | 34 | 37 | 40 | cm |
| C) Underbust Circumference | 28.25 | 32.25 | 36.25 | 40.25 | 44.25 | 48.25 | 52.25 | 56.25 | 60.25 | 64.25 | in |
|  | 73 | 83 | 93 | 103 | 113 | 123 | 134 | 144 | 154 | 164 | cm |
| D) Ruffle Circumference | 56.75 | 64.75 | 72.75 | 80.75 | 88.75 | 96.75 | 104.75 | 112.75 | 120.75 | 128.75 | in |
|  | 145 | 165 | 185 | 206 | 226 | 246 | 267 | 287 | 307 | 327 | cm |
| E) Ruffle Length | 9 | 9 | 9 | 10 | 10 | 10 | 11 | 11 | 12 | 13 | in |
|  | 23 | 23 | 23 | 26 | 26 | 26 | 28 | 28 | 31 | 34 | cm |

The top is designed with 0 to 2 inches (0 to 5 cm) of neutral to positive ease at the underbust. The amount of ease at the breasts depends on your preferred coverage, although -2 to 0 inches (-5 to 0 cm) of negative to neutral ease is recommended.

To select your size, use a measuring tape to take two measurements: 1) the width of one breast (from your side to the center of your chest) and 2) your underbust (the circumference of your chest directly under your breasts). Using the measurements for A and C in the sizing chart above, select the size that best corresponds with your measurements.

If there is a significant difference between your personal measurements and the chart, I recommend casting on the size based on your breast measurement (A). Once you reach the point in the pattern where you will be casting on sts for the back, you will cast on the number of sts that will result in your chosen size for the underbust hem (C). Details regarding that customization will be found in the Underbust Hem section. If a custom size is selected, you may require more or less yarn than what the yarn estimates indicate.

# SCHEMATIC

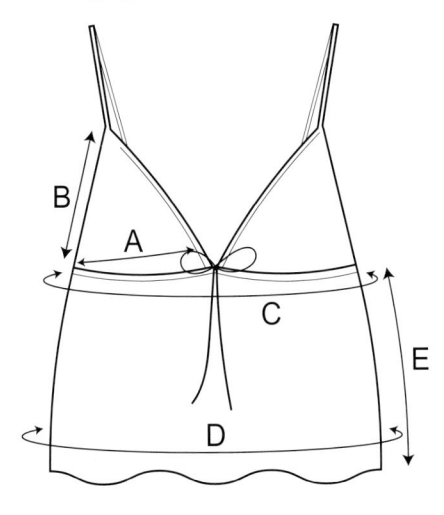

**Feminine & Flirty**

# PETUNIA TOP PATTERN

## FRONT RIGHT

Using US 5 (3.75 mm) needles and holding two strands of yarn, cast on 30 (36, 41, 47, 52) (58, 63, 69, 74, 80) sts using the longtail cast on method.

**Row 1 (RS):** (K1, p1) twice, ssk, k until last 6 sts, k2tog, (p1, k1) twice. [28 (34, 39, 45, 50) (56, 61, 67, 72, 78) sts rem, 2 sts decreased]

**Row 2 (WS):** (P1, k1) twice, p until last 4 sts, (k1, p1) twice.

**Row 3:** (K1, p1) twice, k until last 4 sts, (p1, k1) twice.

**Row 4:** (P1, k1) twice, p until last 4 sts, (k1, p1) twice.

Repeat rows 1–4 a total of 3 (3, 4, 4, 5) (5, 6, 6, 7, 7) more times until 22 (28, 31, 37, 40) (46, 49, 55, 58, 64) sts rem.

**Row 1 (RS):** (K1, p1) twice, ssk, k until last 6 sts, k2tog, (p1, k1) twice. [20 (26, 29, 35, 38) (44, 47, 53, 56, 62) sts rem, 2 sts decreased]

**Row 2 (WS):** (P1, k1) twice, p until last 4 sts, (k1, p1) twice.

**Row 3:** (K1, p1) twice, ssk, k until last 4 sts, (p1, k1) twice. [19 (25, 28, 34, 37) (43, 46, 52, 55, 61) sts rem, 1 st decreased]

**Row 4:** (P1, k1) twice, p until last 4 sts, (k1, p1) twice.

Repeat rows 1–4 a total of 3 (5, 6, 8, 9) (11, 12, 14, 15, 17) more times until 10 sts rem.

**Row 1 (RS):** K1, p1, k1, ssk, k2tog, k1, p1, k1. [8 sts rem, 2 sts decreased]

**Row 2 (WS):** P1, k1, p4, k1, p1.

**Row 3:** K1, p1, ssk, k2tog, p1, k1. [6 sts rem, 2 sts decreased]

**Row 4:** P1, k1, p2, k1, p1.

**Row 5:** K1, ssk, k2tog, k1. [4 sts rem, 2 sts decreased]

**Row 6:** P4.

**Row 7:** Ssk, k2tog. [2 sts rem, 2 sts decreased]

Do not flip work. Switch to shorter needles or DPNs.

**Next row:** Slide 2 sts to end of the needle and k2.

Repeat last row until strap measures 13 inches (33 cm). Bind off and set aside.

## FRONT LEFT

Using US 5 (3.75 mm) needles and holding two strands of yarn, cast on 30 (36, 41, 47, 52) (58, 63, 69, 74, 80) sts using the longtail cast on method.

**Row 1 (RS):** (K1, p1) twice, ssk, k until last 6 sts, k2tog, (p1, k1) twice. [28 (34, 39, 45, 50) (56, 61, 67, 72, 78) sts rem, 2 sts decreased]

**Row 2 (WS):** (P1, k1) twice, p until last 4 sts, (k1, p1) twice.

**Row 3:** (K1, p1) twice, k until last 4 sts, (p1, k1) twice.

**Row 4:** (P1, k1) twice, p until last 4 sts, (k1, p1) twice.

Repeat rows 1–4 a total of 3 (3, 4, 4, 5) (5, 6, 6, 7, 7) more times until 22 (28, 31, 37, 40) (46, 49, 55, 58, 64) sts rem.

**Row 1 (RS):** (K1, p1) twice, ssk, k until last 6 sts, k2tog, (p1, k1) twice. [20 (26, 29, 35, 38) (44, 47, 53, 56, 62) sts rem, 2 sts decreased]

**Row 2 (WS):** (P1, k1) twice, p until last 4 sts, (k1, p1) twice.

**Row 3:** (K1, p1) twice, k until last 6 sts, k2tog, (p1, k1) twice. [19 (25, 28, 34, 37) (43, 46, 52, 55, 61) sts rem, 1 st decreased]

**Row 4:** (P1, k1) twice, p until last 4 sts, (k1, p1) twice.

Repeat rows 1–4 a total of 3 (5, 6, 8, 9) (11, 12, 14, 15, 17) more times until 10 sts rem.

**Row 1 (RS):** K1, p1, k1, ssk, k2tog, k1, p1, k1. [8 sts rem, 2 sts decreased]

**Row 2 (WS):** P1, k1, p4, k1, p1.

**Row 3:** K1, p1, ssk, k2tog, p1, k1. [6 sts rem, 2 sts decreased]

**Row 4:** P1, k1, p2, k1, p1.

**Row 5:** K1, ssk, k2tog, k1. [4 sts rem, 2 sts decreased]

**Row 6:** P4.

**Row 7:** Ssk, k2tog. [2 sts rem, 2 sts decreased]

Do not flip work. Switch to shorter needles or DPNs.

**Next row:** Slide 2 sts to end of the needle and k2.

Repeat last row until strap measures 13 inches (33 cm). Bind off and set aside.

## UNDERBUST HEM

Position your front pieces so they are upside down with the RS facing you. You will now be picking up sts from the bottom edge of each front piece and casting on sts for the back hem. You will begin by picking up sts from the front left piece, casting on sts for the back hem, then picking up sts from the front right piece. You will be working flat.

If you wish to size up or down from your cast on measurement for the bra cups, this is where the modifications will begin. In order to do so, you will be replacing the underlined numbers below and instead cast on the number of sts that will result in your preferred underbust hem size. This new number is the difference between the stitches for your desired underbust hem size and the cup size that you have already knit.

The table on the following page will give you the exact number of sts to cast on. To use it, look at the far-left side to find the size that you casted on for your cups, and then move horizontally to the right until you reach your desired underbust hem size.

**Feminine & Flirty**

**Example 1:** If you casted on size XS for the cups but wish to knit a size L underbust hem, you will need to cast on 160 sts.

**Example 2:** If you casted on size L for the cups but wish to knit a size 3XL underbust hem, you will need to cast on 192 sts.

**NOTE:** *The remainder of the pattern will be knit according to the new custom size you have selected, which means the stitch counts will not match the pattern.*

## Stitches to Cast On for Underbust Hem

### DESIRED HEM SIZE

|     | XS  | S   | M   | L   | XL  | 2XL | 3XL | 4XL | 5XL | 6XL |
|-----|-----|-----|-----|-----|-----|-----|-----|-----|-----|-----|
| XS  | 94  | 116 | 138 | 160 | 182 | 204 | 226 | 248 | 270 | 292 |
| S   | 82  | 104 | 126 | 148 | 170 | 192 | 214 | 236 | 258 | 280 |
| M   | 72  | 94  | 116 | 138 | 160 | 182 | 204 | 226 | 248 | 270 |
| L   | 60  | 82  | 104 | 126 | 148 | 170 | 192 | 214 | 236 | 258 |
| XL  | 50  | 72  | 94  | 116 | 138 | 160 | 182 | 204 | 226 | 248 |
| 2XL | 38  | 60  | 82  | 104 | 126 | 148 | 170 | 192 | 214 | 236 |
| 3XL | 28  | 50  | 72  | 94  | 116 | 138 | 160 | 182 | 204 | 226 |
| 4XL | 16  | 38  | 60  | 82  | 104 | 126 | 148 | 170 | 192 | 214 |
| 5XL | 6   | 28  | 50  | 72  | 94  | 116 | 138 | 160 | 182 | 204 |
| 6XL | -   | 16  | 38  | 60  | 82  | 104 | 126 | 148 | 170 | 192 |

## SET-UP ROW

Using US 5 (3.75 mm) needles and holding one strand of yarn, pick up and k30 (36, 41, 47, 52) (58, 63, 69, 74, 80) from the front left, use the backwards loop method and cast on 94 (104, 116, 126, 138) (148, 160, 170, 182, 192) sts for the back, pick up and k30 (36, 41, 47, 52) (58, 63, 69, 74, 80) from the front right. [154 (176, 198, 220, 242) (264, 286, 308, 330, 352) sts]

**Row 1 (WS):** P all sts.

**Row 2 (RS):** K all sts.

**Rows 3–4:** Repeat rows 1–2.

**Rows 5–7:** P all sts.

**Row 8:** K all sts.

**Row 9:** P all sts.

**Rows 10–11:** Repeat rows 8–9.

### Create Folded Hem

**Row 12 (RS):** Fold your work so the purl row is now the bottom edge. Pick up the corresponding st from the cast on edge and place on left needle. K it together with the st from the current round. Repeat until end.

Bind off all sts loosely.

**TIP:** *You can use a larger needle to assist you in binding off loosely.*

## RUFFLE

You will now be picking up sts for the ruffle, working flat for the set up row before connecting your work to knit in the round. Switch to US 7 (4.5 mm) needles, continuing with one strand of yarn only.

**Set-up row 1 (RS):** Pick up and k154 (176, 198, 220, 242) (264, 286, 308, 330, 352) sts from the purl row of the underbust hem. If you are knitting a custom size, you will be picking up and knitting 1 st per purl st.

**Set-up row 2 (WS):** P all sts.

### Join for Knitting in the Round

**Round 1:** K154 (176, 198, 220, 242) (264, 286, 308, 330, 352), then use the backwards loop method and cast on 1 st. Pm and join for working in the round. [155 (177, 199, 221, 243) (265, 287, 309, 331, 353) sts]

> **NOTE:** *If you are knitting a custom size, you will still need to cast on the 1 st to separate the left and right cups.*

**Round 2:** K all sts.

**Round 3:** *K1, m1l; rep from * until end. [310 (354, 398, 442, 486) (530, 574, 618, 662, 706) sts]

K all rounds until ruffle measures 9 (9, 9, 10, 10) (10, 11, 11, 12, 13)" / 23 (23, 23, 26, 26) (26, 28, 28, 31, 34) cm from the pick up edge. Bind off loosely.

### Joining Straps

With the RS facing, use horizontal invisible seaming technique to join the straps to the back hem.

### I-Cord Tie

Using US 4 (3.5 mm) needles and holding two strands together, cast on 2 sts. Do not turn your needle.

**Next row:** Slide the 2 sts to the other end of your needle and k2.

Repeat last row until I-cord tie reaches 52 (56, 60, 64, 68) (72, 76, 80, 84, 88)" / 133 (143, 153, 163, 173) (183, 194, 204, 214, 224) cm. Bind off and weave in any loose ends.

## FINISHING

Weave in any loose ends. Block your project using your preferred method. Using a safety pin, feed one end of the I-cord into the underbust hem until you reach the other side.

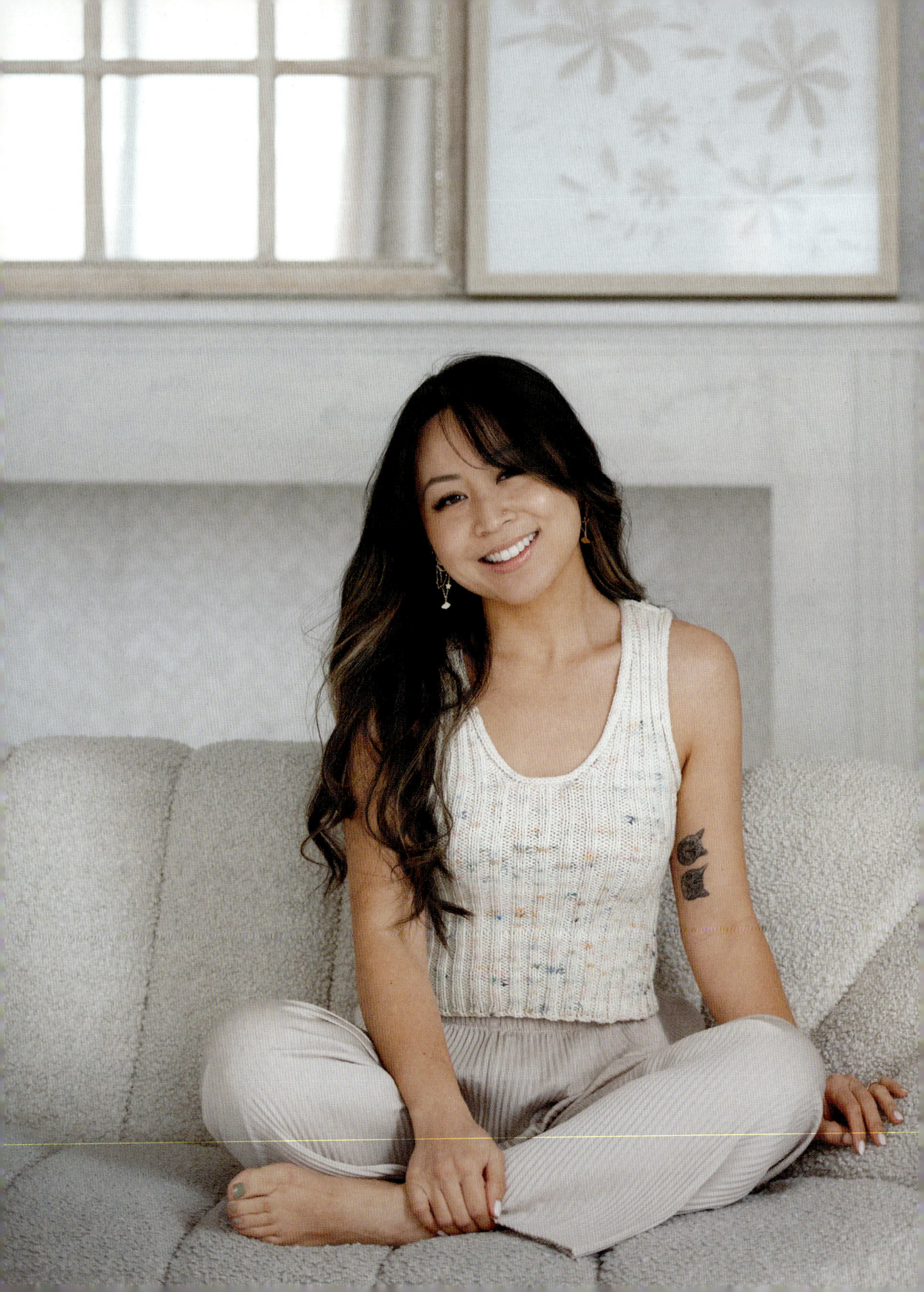

# Knit + Athleisure = Knitleisure

## Knits for Lounging & Staying Active

As a homebody who spends an inordinate amount of time in loungewear, designing a set of patterns that truly reflects my everyday wardrobe was bound to happen sooner or later. While comfort is always a priority across all my designs, I wanted knitwear that also looked the part. As nice as it is to make and wear knitwear for special occasions, knitting your own activewear and loungewear is an underrated endeavor.

The result? A set of garments you can truly live in: Clothes meant to be worn so frequently that you'll want to make multiple versions just so you'll have one on rotation at all times. Clothes that you can wear while curled up on the couch in the morning and not have to change out of to get to the pickleball court in the afternoon.

The patterns in this collection all have design elements catered towards practicality and wearability. The matching Pocket set is my take on the classic lounge set: The oversized, boxy fit of the Poppy Pocket Tee (page 53) and the drawstring waistband of the Poppy Pocket Shorts (page 65) are all features that prioritize comfort and coziness. By combining basic stitches with eye-catching details like pockets with a snap-on enclosure, craftsmanship and quality are never an afterthought. The pockets also add another level of functionality on top of the otherwise straightforward construction.

If you're looking for a sleeveless option, the all-around ribbing of the Wisteria Tank (page 75) creates a soft, stretchy fabric that will accentuate your curves without feeling constricting. The Iris Racerback Tank (page 45) is also the perfect top to wear on the go, whether you're out running errands or off to a light yoga session. The racerback detail, elegant waist shaping and folded hem finishing are all key to its simple sophistication. Whether the plan is to lounge at home or head on over to the gym, these pieces will take you from home wear to day wear without breaking a sweat.

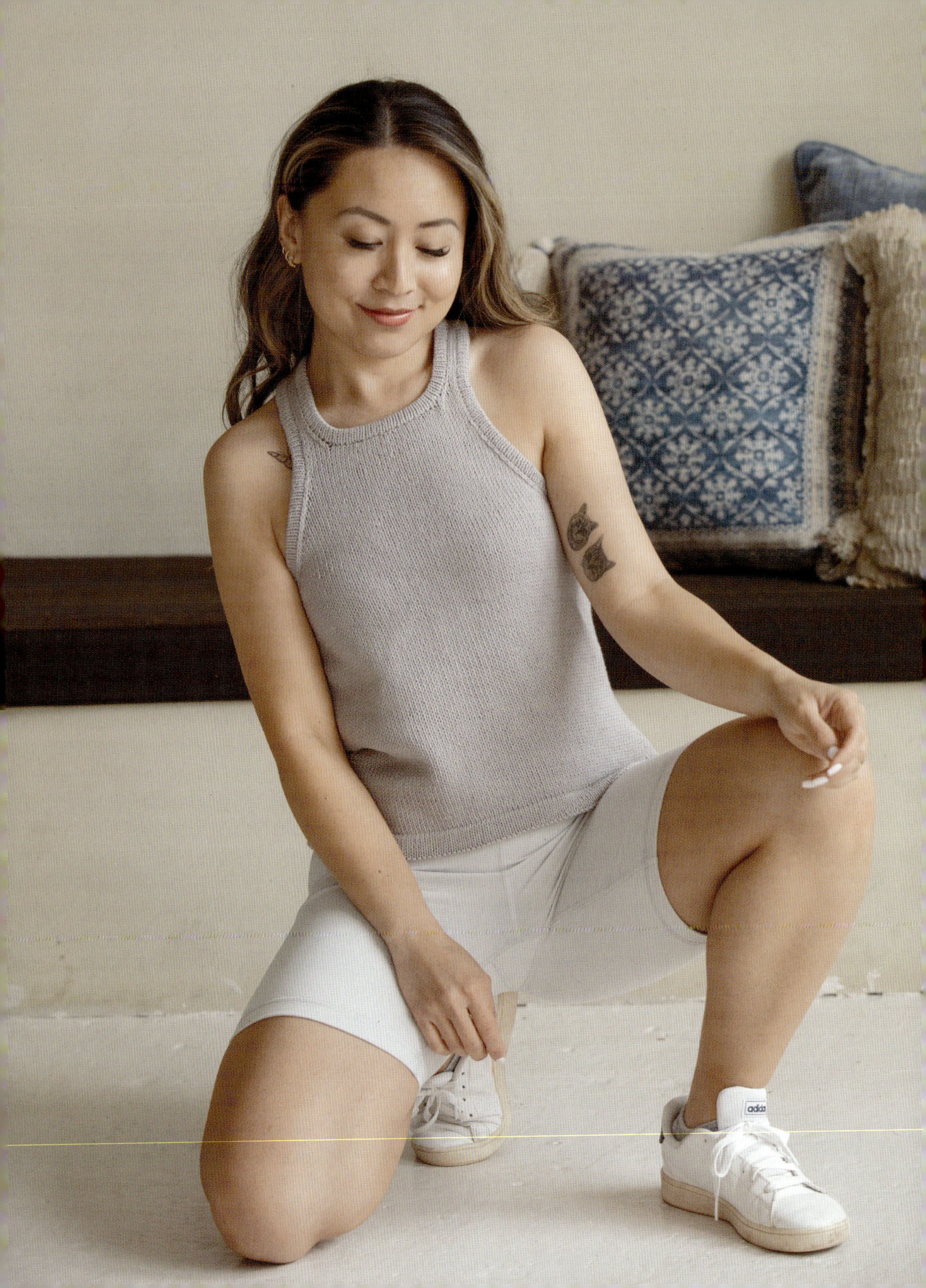
adidas

# Iris Racerback Tank

Meet your new everyday essential. The Iris Racerback Tank is a classic racerback tank you can wear nearly everywhere, be it the gym, beach or mall. Knit with a sport weight cotton, the result is a lightweight garment that you'll be able to stay cool and comfortable in throughout the day. The classic racerback cut reveals the shoulder blades, allowing the wearer to move with ease. Whether you're wearing it oversized over a sports bra or prefer it fitted, you'll want to make these in multiple colors for whatever mood you're in that day.

## Construction Notes

The tank is worked in the round from the bottom up, beginning with a folded hem. Waist decreases and bust increases are worked into the body for a feminine silhouette. The body is continued in the round until separating for the front and back pieces. The front pieces are further separated into left and right sections for neck shaping. The back piece is then worked flat with decreases on both sides to create the racerback shape before joining with the front straps. Finally, stitches are picked up for both the armhole and neck edge, folded inwards and seamed to the pick up edge for a clean finish.

## SKILL LEVEL

Intermediate

## SIZING

XS (S, M, L, XL) (2XL, 3XL, 4XL, 5XL, 6XL)

Bust circumference of 29 (32.5, 37, 41, 45) (48.5, 53, 57, 60.5, 65)" / 74 (83, 94, 104, 114) (124, 135, 145, 154, 165) cm, blocked

## Materials

### Yarn

Sport weight, Drops Safran in 07 (100% cotton), 175 yds (160 m) per 50-g skein

An alternate sample was also knit with Drops Safran in 18.

Any sport weight yarn can be used for this pattern as long as it matches gauge.

## Yardage/Meterage

495 (575, 685, 755, 870) (930, 1040, 1260, 1370, 1445) yds / 450 (525, 625, 690, 795) (850, 950, 1150, 1250, 1320) m of sport weight yarn

## Needles

**For hem:** US 3 (3.25 mm), 16- to 47-inch (40- to 120-cm) circular needle

**For body:** US 4 (3.5 mm), 24- to 60-inch (60- to 150-cm) circular needle

**For neckband and armhole edge:** US 4 (3.5 mm), 16- to 24-inch (40- to 60-cm) circular needle

## Notions

Scrap yarn or stitch holder

Scissors

Stitch markers

Tapestry needle

## GAUGE

27 sts x 32 rounds = 4 inches (10 cm) in stockinette st worked both flat and in the round using larger needles (blocked)

## TECHNIQUES

Kitchener Stitch (or 3-Needle Bind Off [page 146])

Whip Stitch (page 150)

# ABBREVIATIONS

| | |
|---|---|
| 0 or - | no stitch / step does not apply to your size |
| BOR | beginning of round |
| dec | decrease |
| inc | increase |
| k | knit |
| k2tog | knit 2 sts together [1 st decreased] |
| m1l | make 1 left: use the left needle to pick up the strand between the last worked st and the next unworked st from front to back, knit this st through the back loop [1 st increased] |
| m1r | make 1 right: use the left needle to pick up the strand between the last worked st and the next unworked st from back to front, knit this st through the front loop [1 st increased] |
| p | purl |
| patt | pattern |
| pm | place marker |
| rem | remain(ing) |
| rep | repeat |
| RS | right side |
| sm | slip marker |
| ssk | slip 2 sts knitwise, one at a time; move both stitches back to the left needle; knit these 2 sts together through the back loops [1 st decreased] |
| st(s) | stitch(es) |
| stm | stitch marker |
| work(ing) even | continue working the pattern as established without any increases or decreases |

Light & Breezy Knitwear

# SCHEMATIC SIZING CHART

|  | XS | S | M | L | XL | 2XL | 3XL | 4XL | 5XL | 6XL |  |
|---|---|---|---|---|---|---|---|---|---|---|---|
| A) Body Circumference | 29 | 32.5 | 37 | 41 | 45 | 48.5 | 53 | 57 | 60.5 | 65 | in |
|  | 74 | 83 | 94 | 104 | 114 | 124 | 135 | 145 | 154 | 165 | cm |
| B) Armhole Depth | 8.5 | 8.75 | 9.75 | 9.75 | 10.5 | 11 | 11.5 | 12.25 | 12.75 | 12.75 | in |
|  | 22 | 22 | 25 | 25 | 27 | 28 | 29 | 31 | 33 | 33 | cm |
| C) Shoulder Width | 7.25 | 8.75 | 10 | 10.75 | 12.25 | 12.5 | 13.5 | 14.75 | 16 | 16.25 | in |
|  | 19 | 22 | 26 | 27 | 31 | 32 | 34 | 38 | 41 | 41 | cm |
| D) Body Length from Underarm to Hem | 11 | 11.5 | 12 | 12 | 12.5 | 13 | 13 | 13.5 | 13.5 | 14 | in |
|  | 28 | 29 | 31 | 31 | 32 | 33 | 33 | 34 | 34 | 36 | cm |
| E) Garment Length | 19 | 19.75 | 21.25 | 21.25 | 22.5 | 23.5 | 24 | 25.25 | 25.75 | 26.25 | in |
|  | 48 | 50 | 54 | 54 | 57 | 60 | 61 | 64 | 66 | 67 | cm |

WS     wrong side

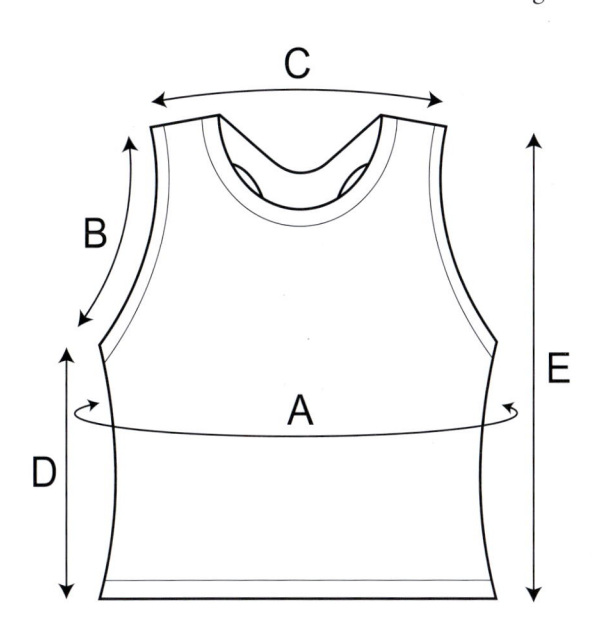

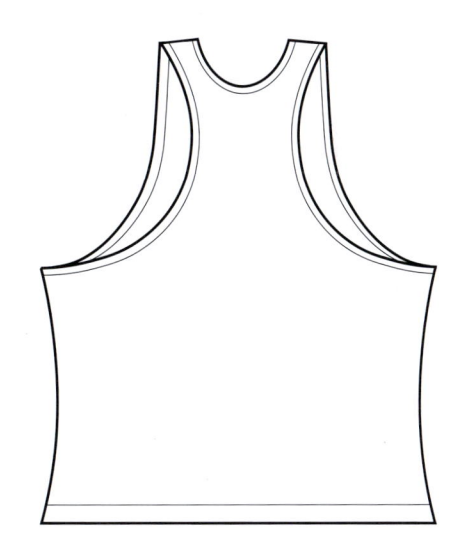

Knit + Athleisure = Knitleisure

The top is designed with -1.5 to 1.5 inches (-4 to 4 cm) of negative to positive ease. Sample shown is knit in size XS.

# IRIS RACERBACK TANK PATTERN

## BODY

Using US 3 (3.25 mm) needles, cast on 196 (212, 232, 260, 284) (312, 340, 352, 372, 392) sts using the longtail cast on method. Pm and join for working in the round.

**Rounds 1–6:** K all sts.

**Round 7 (turning round):** P all sts.

**Rounds 8–14:** K all sts.

## Create Folded Hem

Fold your work so the purl round is now the bottom edge. Pick up the corresponding st from the cast on edge and place on left needle. K it together with the st from the current round. Repeat until end.

Switch to US 4 (3.5 mm) needles.

**Next round:** K98 (106, 116, 130, 142) (156, 170, 176, 186, 196), pm for side, k98 (106, 116, 130, 142) (156, 170, 176, 186, 196).

K all rounds until piece measures 1.75 inches (4 cm) from the bottom of the folded hem.

## Begin Waist Decreases

**Round 1 (dec):** *K6, ssk, k until 8 sts before side stm, k2tog, k6; sm and rep from * one more time. [192 (208, 228, 256, 280) (308, 336, 348, 368, 388) sts rem, 4 sts decreased]

**Rounds 2–4:** K all sts.

Repeat rounds 1–4 a total of 5 (5, 4, 4, 4) (6, 6, 5, 4, 5) more times until 172 (188, 212, 240, 264) (284, 312, 328, 352, 368) sts rem.

Work even until piece measures 5 (5, 5, 6, 6) (6, 6, 6, 6, 6)" / 13 (13, 13, 14, 14) (14, 16, 15, 15, 15) cm from the bottom of the folded hem.

## Begin Bust Increases

*Sizes XS & S only*

**Round 1 (inc):** *K6, m1r, k until 6 sts before side stm, m1l, k6; sm and rep from * one more time. [176 (192, -, -, -) (-, -, -, -, -) sts, 4 sts increased]

**Rounds 2–8:** K all sts.

Repeat rounds 1–8 a total of 3 (5, -, -, -) (-, -, -, -, -) more times until there are 188 (212, -, -, -) (-, -, -, -, -) sts.

*Sizes M–XL only*

**Round 1 (inc):** *K6, m1r, k until 6 sts before side stm, m1l, k6; sm and rep from * one more time. [- (-, 216, 244, 268) (-, -, -, -, -), 4 sts increased]

**Rounds 2–6:** K all sts.

Repeat rounds 1–6 a total of - (-, 6, 5, 6) (-, -, -, -, -) more times until there are - (-, 240, 264, 292) (-, -, -, -, -) sts.

*Sizes 2XL–6XL only*

**Round 1 (inc):** *K6, m1r, k until 6 sts before side stm, m1l, k6; sm and rep from * one more time. [- (-, -, -, -) (288, 316, 332, 356, 372), 4 sts increased]

**Rounds 2–4:** K all sts.

Repeat rounds 1–4 a total of - (-, -, -, -) (7, 7, 10, 10, 13) more times until there are - (-, -, -, -) (316, 344, 372, 396, 424) sts.

*All sizes resume*
Work even until piece measures 11 (11.5, 12, 12, 12.5) (13, 13, 13.5, 13.5, 14)" /28 (29, 30, 30, 32) (33, 33, 34, 34, 36) cm from the bottom of the folded hem.

**Next row:** Remove BOR stm. Bind off 6 (6, 6, 8, 8) (8, 10, 10, 10, 12) sts, work in patt until side stm. Remove side stm and turn. Leave rem 94 (106, 120, 132, 146) (158, 172, 186, 198, 212) sts on a holder or spare yarn to return to later. [88 (100, 114, 124, 138) (150, 162, 176, 188, 200) sts rem]

## FRONT
**Next row (WS):** Bind off 6 (6, 6, 8, 8) (8, 10, 10, 10, 12) sts, p until end. [82 (94, 108, 116, 130) (142, 152, 166, 178, 188) sts rem]

**Next row (RS):** Bind off 5 (5, 5, 6, 6) (8, 8, 8, 8, 10) sts, k until end. [77 (89, 103, 110, 124) (134, 144, 158, 170, 178) sts rem]

**Next row:** Bind off 5 (5, 5, 6, 6) (8, 8, 8, 8, 10) sts, p until end. [72 (84, 98, 104, 118) (126, 136, 150, 162, 168) sts rem]

**Next row:** Bind off 4 (4, 4, 5, 5) (7, 7, 7, 7, 9) sts, k until end. [68 (80, 94, 99, 113) (119, 129, 143, 155, 159) sts rem]

**Next row:** Bind off 4 (4, 4, 5, 5) (7, 7, 7, 7, 9) sts, p until end. [64 (76, 90, 94, 108) (112, 122, 136, 148, 150) sts rem]

**Next row (dec):** K1, ssk, k until last 3 sts, k2tog, k1. [62 (74, 88, 92, 106) (110, 120, 134, 146, 148) sts rem, 2 sts decreased]

**Next row:** P all sts.

Repeat last 2 rows a total of 9 (10, 12, 12, 13) (14, 15, 16, 18, 18) more times until 44 (54, 64, 68, 80) (82, 90, 102, 110, 112) sts rem.

**Row 1 (RS, dec):** K1, ssk, k until last 3 sts, k2tog, k1. [42 (52, 62, 66, 78) (80, 88, 100, 108, 110) sts rem, 2 sts decreased]

**Row 2 (WS):** P all sts.

**Row 3:** K all sts.

**Row 4:** P all sts.

Repeat rows 1–4 a total of 1 (1, 2, 2, 3) (3, 4, 5, 5, 5) more time(s) until 40 (50, 58, 62, 72) (74, 80, 90, 98, 100) sts rem.

Work even until piece measures 15.5 (16.25, 17.75, 17.75, 19) (20, 20.5, 21.75, 22.25,

19) sts remaining on each side of the bindoff sts. Leave rem left front sts on a holder or spare yarn to return to later.

## FRONT RIGHT
**Row 1 (WS):** P all sts.

**Row 2 (RS):** K1, ssk, k until end. [6 (10, 12, 12, 14) (14, 16, 18, 18, 18) sts rem, 1 st decreased]

Repeat rows 1–2 a total of 1 (5, 7, 5, 7) (7, 7, 9, 9, 9) more time(s) until 5 (5, 5, 7, 7) (7, 9, 9, 9, 9) sts rem.

Work even until piece measures 19 (19.75, 21.25, 21.25, 22.5) (23.5, 24, 25.25, 25.75, 26.25)" / 48 (50, 54, 54, 57) (59, 61, 64, 65, 67) cm from the bottom of the folded hem. Break yarn and move sts to a holder or spare yarn to return to later.

> **TIP:** Make a note on whether your final row ended on the RS/WS so the Front Left can match perfectly.

## FRONT LEFT
Move live sts back to US 4 (3.5 mm) needles and rejoin yarn to WS of work.

**Row 1 (WS):** P all sts.

**Row 2 (RS):** K until last 3 sts, k2tog, k1. [6 (10, 12, 12, 14) (14, 16, 17, 17, 17) sts rem, 1 st decreased]

Repeat rows 1–2 a total of 1 (5, 7, 5, 7) (7, 7, 9, 9, 9) more time(s) until 5 (5, 5, 7, 7) (7, 9, 9, 9, 9) sts rem.

Work even until piece measures 19 (19.75, 21.25, 21.25, 22.5) (23.5, 24, 25.25, 25.75,

22.75)" / 39 (41, 45, 45, 48) (50, 52, 55, 57, 58) cm from the bottom of the folded hem. Your last row should be a WS row.

## NECKLINE
You will now begin by binding off stitches across the center for the base of the neck, then work each side of the neckline shaping separately, ending with the top of the strap where stitches are placed on hold.

**Next row (RS):** K7 (11, 13, 13, 15) (15, 17, 19, 19, 19), loosely bind off 26 (28, 32, 36, 42) (44, 46, 52, 60, 62) sts, k until end. You will have 7 (11, 13, 13, 15) (15, 17, 19, 19,

Light & Breezy Knitwear

26.25)" / 48 (50, 54, 54, 57) (59, 61, 64, 65, 67) cm from the bottom of the folded hem. Break yarn and move sts to a holder or spare yarn to return to later.

## BACK
Move live sts back to US 4 (3.5 mm) needles and rejoin yarn to RS of work.

**Row 1 (RS):** Bind off 33 (38, 41, 47, 51) (55, 60, 64, 68, 75) sts, k until end. [61 (68, 79, 85, 95) (103, 112, 122, 130, 137) sts rem]

**Row 2 (WS):** Bind off 33 (38, 41, 47, 51) (55, 60, 64, 68, 75) sts, p until end. [28 (30, 38, 38, 44) (48, 52, 58, 62, 62) sts rem]

**Row 3 (dec):** K1, ssk, k until last 3 sts, k2tog, k1. [26 (28, 36, 36, 42) (46, 50, 56, 60, 60) sts rem, 2 sts decreased]

**Row 4:** P all sts.

Repeat rows 3–4 a total of 8 (9, 13, 12, 15) (17, 18, 21, 23, 23) more times until 10 (10, 10, 12, 12) (12, 14, 14, 14, 14) sts rem.

**Next row (RS):** K all sts.

**Next row (WS):** P all sts.

**Next row (inc):** K2, m1r, k until last 2 sts, m1l, k2. [12 (12, 12, 14, 14) (14, 16, 16, 16, 16) sts, 2 sts increased]

**Next row:** P all sts.

Repeat last 2 rows a total of 3 (3, 3, 4, 4) (4, 5, 5, 5, 5) more times until you have 18 (18, 18, 22, 22) (22, 26, 26, 26, 26) sts.

**Next row (RS):** K7 (7, 7, 9, 9) (9, 11, 11, 11, 11), bind off 4 sts, k7 (7, 7, 9, 9) (9, 11, 11, 11, 11).

Move Back Right sts on a spare needle or scrap yarn to return to later.

## BACK LEFT
**Next row (WS):** P all sts.

**Next row (RS):** K1, ssk, k until end. [6 (6, 6, 8, 8) (8, 10, 10, 10, 10) sts rem]

**Next row:** P all sts.

**Next row:** K1, ssk, k until end. [5 (5, 5, 7, 7) (7, 9, 9, 9, 9) sts rem]

**Next row:** P all sts.

Work even until piece measures 19 (19.75, 21.25, 21.25, 22.5) (23.5, 24, 25.25, 25.75, 26.25)" / 48 (50, 54, 54, 57) (59, 61, 64, 65, 67) cm from the bottom of the folded hem. Break yarn, leaving a 14-inch (36-cm) tail for joining later to the front. Move live sts to a holder or spare yarn to return to later.

## BACK RIGHT
Rejoin yarn to WS of work.

**Next row (WS):** P all sts.

**Next row (RS):** K until last 3 sts, k2tog, k1. [6 (6, 6, 8, 8) (8, 10, 10, 10, 10) sts rem]

**Next row:** P all sts.

**Next row:** K until last 3 sts, k2tog, k1. [5 (5, 5, 7, 7) (7, 9, 9, 9, 9) sts rem]

**Next row:** P all sts.

Work even until piece measures 19 (19.75, 21.25, 21.25, 22.5) (23.5, 24, 25.25, 25.75, 26.25)" / 48 (50, 54, 54, 57) (59, 61, 64, 65, 67) cm from the bottom of the folded hem. Break yarn, leaving a 14-inch (36-cm) tail for joining later to the front.

### Joining the Straps
With the WS facing each other, use the Kitchener stitch (or 3-needle bind off) to seam the left front strap to the left back strap and the right front strap to the right back strap. Weave in any loose ends. At this point, the straps will look very flimsy prior to picking up sts for the hem—trust the process!

> **TIP:** *Weave in ends closer to the edge of the garment because the folded hems of the neckband and armhole edge will hide the ends.*

### NECKBAND

Using US 3 (3.25 mm) needles and beginning at the base of the right back strap, pick up and k4 from the back neck, then pick up and k3 out of every 4 sts down the left neck, evenly pick up and k3 out of every 4 sts from the front, then pick up and k3 out of every 4 sts up the strap and back towards the racerback. Pm and join for knitting in the round.

K for 8 rounds. Loosely bind off and break yarn, leaving a tail 2x the circumference of the neck. Fold the neckband inwards and whip stitch the bind off edge to the pick up edge.

> **TIP:** *You can use a larger needle to assist you in binding loosely.*

### ARMHOLE EDGE (MAKE 2)

Using US 3 (3.25 mm) needles and beginning at the center of the underarm, evenly pick up and k3 out of every 4 sts up towards the shoulder and back down to the underarm. Pm and join for knitting in the round.

K for 8 rounds. Loosely bind off and break yarn, leaving a tail 2x the circumference of the armhole. Fold the armhole edge inwards and whip stitch the bind off edge to the pick up edge.

Repeat for the other armhole edge.

### FINISHING

Weave in any loose ends. Block your project using your preferred method.

# Poppy Pocket Tee

Oversized tees are the new year-round staple. Whether worn with shorts in the summer or layered with your favorite cardigan in cooler months, the boxy, wide-cut body and sleeves make for a comfortable look regardless of setting or season. An oversized knit tee occupies a unique space in modern fashion: It is simultaneously trendy *and* will never go out of style.

What distinguishes this from your basic tee is its defining feature: a single pocket with a classic flap enclosure. The seamless inset pocket is knit in a contrasting color, which creates a fun little detail among the stockinette fabric. Snap-on buttons are installed on the wrong side of the flap to ensure it stays in place, giving it a clean and refined look. This project knits up quickly and will most definitely be one of your go-to pieces for days when you don't want to worry about piecing together an outfit. You'll be making a low-key casual style statement no matter what.

## Construction Notes

*The tee is worked in the round from the bottom up beginning with a folded hem. The top is later separated into front and back pieces and worked flat. Once the appropriate length is reached for the front, you will begin working on the pocket using a contrasting yarn (or the main color, if desired).*

*Once both front and back pieces are completed and seamed, stitches are picked up around the neckline for the neckband. Sleeves are also worked in the round from the top down, incorporating German short rows for shaping. Finally, snap-on buttons are installed after blocking.*

## SKILL LEVEL
Intermediate

## SIZING
XS (S, M, L, XL) (2XL, 3XL, 4XL, 5XL, 6XL)

Bust circumference of 34.25 (38.5, 42.25, 46.5, 50.25) (54.5, 58.25, 62.5, 66.25, 70.5)" / 87 (98, 107, 118, 128) (139, 148, 159, 168, 179) cm, blocked

## Materials

### Yarn

**Main Color (MC):** DK weight, Debbie Bliss Cotton Denim DK in 02 (100% cotton), 218 yds (200 m) per 100-g skein

**Contrast Color (CC):** DK weight, Koigu® Jasmine in J132S (100% wool), 242 yds (221 m) per 100-g skein

Any DK or worsted weight yarn can be used for this pattern as long as it matches gauge.

### Yardage/Meterage

855 (925, 1005, 1100, 1185) (1290, 1400, 1515, 1630, 1750) yds / 785 (850, 920, 1010, 1085) (1185, 1285, 1390, 1495, 1605) m of DK or worsted weight yarn in MC

13 (17, 20, 23, 28) (32, 35, 42, 46, 50) yds / 12 (16, 18, 21, 26) (29, 32, 39, 42, 46) m of DK or worsted weight yarn in CC

### Needles

**For hem:** US 4 (3.5 mm), 24- to 60-inch (60- to 150-cm) circular needles

**For body:** US 6 (4 mm), 24- to 60-inch (60- to 150-cm) circular needles

**For sleeves:** US 6 (4 mm), 16- to 24-inch (40- to 60-cm) circular needles

(Materials continued)

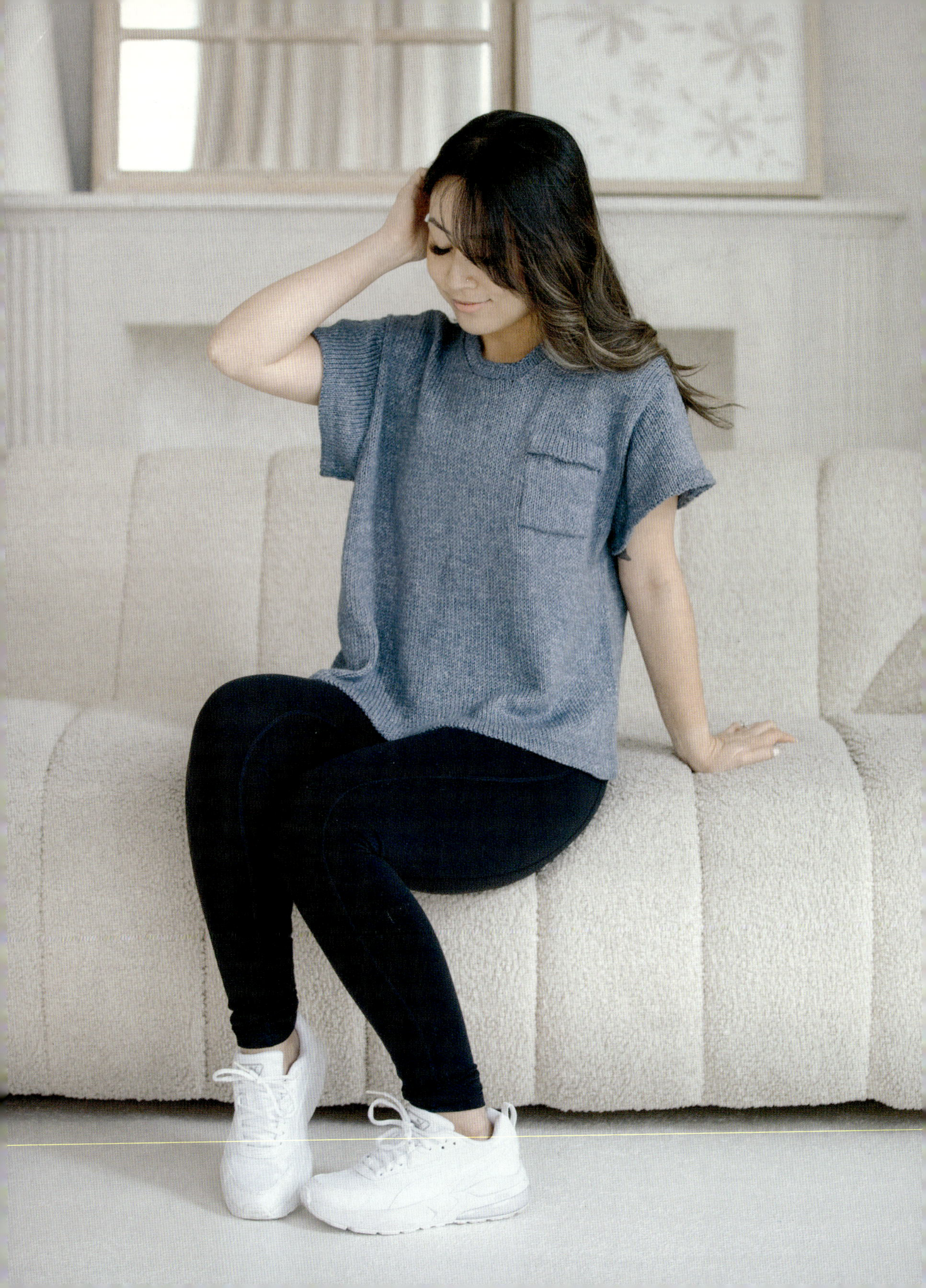

**Notions**

*Removable stitch markers*

*Scrap yarn in a contrasting color*

*1 set of snap-on buttons (8–12 mm, optional)*

*Stitch markers*

*Tapestry needle*

## GAUGE

*22 sts x 27 rows = 4 inches (10 cm) in stockinette st using larger needles (blocked)*

## TECHNIQUES

*German Short Rows (page 151)*

*Horizontal Invisible Seam (page 149)*

*Mattress Stitch (page 150)*

*Whip Stitch (page 150)*

# ABBREVIATIONS

| | |
|---|---|
| BOR | beginning of round |
| CC | contrast color |
| DS | double stitch |
| k | knit |
| k2tog | knit 2 sts together [1 st decreased] |
| MC | main color |
| MDS | make double stitch [see German short rows in Techniques] |
| p | purl |
| patt | pattern |
| pm | place marker |
| rem | remain(ing) |
| RS | right side |
| sm | slip marker |
| ssk | slip 2 sts knitwise, one at a time; move both stitches back to the left needle; knit these 2 sts together through the back loops [1 st decreased] |
| st(s) | stitch(es) |
| stm(s) | stitch marker(s) |
| WS | wrong side |

## SIZING CHART

|  | XS | S | M | L | XL | 2XL | 3XL | 4XL | 5XL | 6XL |  |
|---|---|---|---|---|---|---|---|---|---|---|---|
| A) Body Circumference | 34.25 | 38.5 | 42.25 | 46.5 | 50.25 | 54.5 | 58.25 | 62.5 | 66.25 | 70.5 | in |
|  | 87 | 98 | 107 | 118 | 128 | 138.5 | 148 | 159 | 168 | 179 | cm |
| B) Pocket Width | 3 | 3.25 | 3.25 | 3.75 | 3.75 | 4 | 4 | 4.25 | 4.75 | 5 | in |
|  | 7 | 8 | 8 | 9 | 9 | 10 | 10 | 11 | 12 | 13 | cm |
| C) Pocket Depth | 2.75 | 3.25 | 3.5 | 3.75 | 4.25 | 4.5 | 4.75 | 5.25 | 5.5 | 5.75 | in |
|  | 7 | 8 | 9 | 10 | 11 | 11 | 12 | 13 | 14 | 15 | cm |
| D) Armhole Depth | 9 | 9.5 | 10 | 10.5 | 11 | 11.5 | 12 | 12.5 | 13 | 13.5 | in |
|  | 23 | 24 | 25 | 27 | 28 | 29 | 30 | 32 | 33 | 34 | cm |
| E) Sleeve Circumference | 16 | 17 | 17.75 | 19 | 19.75 | 21.5 | 23 | 24.75 | 25.5 | 25.75 | in |
|  | 41 | 43 | 45 | 48 | 50 | 54 | 58 | 63 | 65 | 66 | cm |
| F) Sleeve Length | 2.75 | 2.75 | 2.75 | 2.75 | 2.75 | 2.75 | 2.75 | 2.75 | 2.75 | 2.75 | in |
|  | 7 | 7 | 7 | 7 | 7 | 7 | 7 | 7 | 7 | 7 | cm |
| G) Garment Length | 20.5 | 21 | 21.5 | 22 | 22.5 | 23 | 23.5 | 24 | 24.5 | 25 | in |
|  | 52 | 53 | 55 | 56 | 57 | 58 | 60 | 61 | 62 | 64 | cm |

The top is designed with 4 to 7 inches (10 to 18 cm) of positive ease. Sample shown is knit in size S with 7 inches (18 cm) of positive ease.

## SCHEMATIC

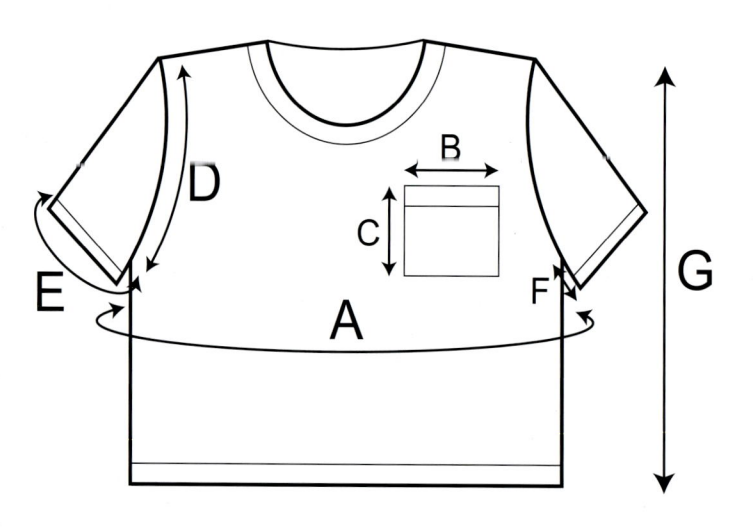

Light & Breezy Knitwear

# POPPY POCKET TEE PATTERN

## BODY
Using US 4 (3.5 mm) needles and MC, cast on 188 (212, 232, 256, 276) (300, 320, 344, 364, 388) sts using the longtail cast on method. Pm and join for working in the round.

**Rounds 1–5:** K all sts

**Round 6:** P all sts

**Rounds 7–12:** K all sts

### Create Folded Hem
Fold your work so the purl round is now the bottom. Pick up the corresponding st from the cast on edge and place on left needle. K it together with the st from the current round. Repeat until you reach the final st.

Switch to US 6 (4 mm) needles.

K all rounds until piece measures 11.5 inches (29 cm) from the bottom of the folded hem (round 6).

### Separate Front/Back
**Row 1 (RS):** Remove BOR stm. Bind off 4 (5, 5, 6, 6) (7, 7, 8, 8, 9) sts, k90 (101, 111, 122, 132) (143, 153, 164, 174, 185). Turn and leave rem 94 (106, 116, 128, 138) (150, 160, 172, 182, 194) sts on a holder or spare yarn to return to later.

**Row 2 (WS):** Bind off 4 (5, 5, 6, 6) (7, 7, 8, 8, 9) sts, p until end. [86 (96, 106, 116, 126) (136, 146, 156, 166, 176) sts rem]

**Row 3:** K1, ssk, k until last 3 sts, k2tog, k1. [84 (94, 104, 114, 124) (134, 144, 154, 164, 174) sts rem, 2 sts decreased]

**Row 4:** P all sts.

Repeat rows 3–4 a total of 5 (5, 6, 7, 7) (8, 9, 9, 10, 11) more times until 74 (84, 92, 100, 110) (118, 126, 136, 144, 152) sts rem.

**Next row (RS):** K all sts.

**Next row (WS):** P all sts.

Repeat last 2 rows until piece measures 15 (15, 15.5, 15.75, 15.75) (16, 16.25, 16.25, 16.5, 16.75)" / 39 (39, 40, 41, 41) (41, 42, 42, 42, 43) cm from the bottom of the folded hem.

### Create Pocket
You will now begin working on the pocket. You will be working flat using CC yarn. Once the appropriate length is reached, you will return to the remainder of the front using MC.

**Next row (RS):** Using MC yarn, k9 (11, 11, 13, 13) (15, 15, 17, 17, 19), do not break MC yarn. Using CC yarn, k16 (18, 18, 20, 20) (22, 22, 24, 26, 28) for the pocket. Turn.

**Next row (WS):** P16 (18, 18, 20, 20) (22, 22, 24, 26, 28).

**Next row:** K16 (18, 18, 20, 20) (22, 22, 24, 26, 28) (Image 1, page 58).

**NOTE:** *You can also knit the pocket with another pair of US 6 (4 mm) needles if that is easier to manage.*

Repeat last 2 rows (working on the pocket only) until the pocket lining reaches 6.5 (7.5, 8, 8.5, 9.5) (10, 10.5, 11.5, 12, 12.5)" / 17 (20, 21, 22, 25) (26, 27, 30, 31, 32) cm. Break CC yarn, leaving a tail long enough for marking where to seam the pocket afterwards (Images 2 & 3, pages 58–59).

## Join Pocket

**Next row (RS):** Return to MC yarn and k16 (18, 18, 20, 20) (22, 22, 24, 26, 28) across the top of the pocket sts. Continue using MC to knit across the rem sts (Images 4 & 5).

## Mark Pocket, Pocket Flap and Snap-on Button Placement

Before continuing with the front, use a tapestry needle and a strand of CC yarn to mark where the pocket will be seamed after (Image 6). Use a removable stm to mark the male side of the snap-on button placement (Image 7). I suggest placing the snap-on button four rows below the beginning of the pocket in the center of the pocket. From the beginning of the RS row, this would be after st 17 (20, 20, 23, 23) (26, 26, 29, 30, 33).

Using a tapestry needle and a strand of CC yarn, insert a lifeline in the row of MC sts right above the pocket to mark where the pocket flap will be picked up afterwards (Image 8).

**Next row (WS):** P all sts.

**Next row:** K all sts.

Repeat last 2 rows until piece measures 16.5 (17, 17.5, 18, 18.5) (19, 19.5, 20, 20.5, 21)" / 42 (44, 45, 46, 47) (49, 50, 51, 53, 54) cm from the bottom of the folded hem. Repeat a WS row one more time.

## Neck Bind Off

**Next row (RS):** K32 (37, 41, 44, 48) (52, 55, 60, 63, 66), bind off 10 (10, 10, 12, 14) (14, 16, 16, 18, 20) sts, k until end.

Move Front Left sts on a spare needle or scrap yarn to return to later.

Image 1

Image 2

Image 3: Once the CC rows are completed, fold the fabric so the RS of the stockinette sts make up the inside of the pocket.

Image 4

Image 5: This is how the pocket looks from the WS of the project.

Image 6

Image 7

Image 8: This is how the pocket looks once the front piece is completed. You will return to the lifeline later for the pocket flap.

Knit + Athleisure = Knitleisure

59

## FRONT RIGHT

**Next row (WS):** P all sts.

**Next row (RS):** K1, ssk, k until end. [31 (36, 40, 43, 47) (51, 54, 59, 62, 65) sts rem, 1 st decreased]

Repeat last 2 rows a total of 8 more times until 23 (28, 32, 35, 39) (43, 46, 51, 54, 57) sts rem.

**Next row (WS):** Bind off 5 (7, 8, 8, 9) (10, 11, 12, 13, 14) sts, p until end. [18 (21, 24, 27, 30) (33, 35, 39, 41, 43) sts rem]

**Next row (RS):** K all sts.

**Next row:** Bind off 6 (7, 8, 9, 10) (11, 11, 13, 13, 14) sts, p until end. [12 (14, 16, 18, 20) (22, 24, 26, 28, 29) sts rem]

**Next row:** K all sts.

**Next row:** Bind off 6 (7, 8, 9, 10) (11, 12, 13, 14, 14) sts, p until end. [6 (7, 8, 9, 10) (11, 12, 13, 14, 15) sts rem]

**Next row:** K all sts.

Bind off rem 6 (7, 8, 9, 10) (11, 12, 13, 14, 15) sts. Break yarn, leaving a tail 2x the length of the shoulder for seaming.

## FRONT LEFT

Rejoin yarn to WS of work.

**Next row (WS):** P all sts.

**Next row (RS):** K until last 3 sts, k2tog, k1. [31 (36, 40, 43, 47) (51, 54, 59, 62, 65) sts rem, 1 st decreased]

Repeat last 2 rows a total of 8 more times until 23 (28, 32, 35, 39) (43, 46, 51, 54, 57) sts rem.

**Next row (WS):** P all sts.

**Next row (RS):** Bind off 5 (7, 8, 8, 9) (10, 11, 12, 13, 14) sts, k until end. [18 (21, 24, 27, 30) (33, 35, 39, 41, 43) sts rem]

**Next row:** P all sts.

**Next row:** Bind off 6 (7, 8, 9, 10) (11, 11, 13, 13, 14) sts, k until end. [12 (14, 16, 18, 20) (22, 24, 26, 28, 29) sts rem]

**Next row:** P all sts.

**Next row:** Bind off 6 (7, 8, 9, 10) (11, 12, 13, 14, 14) sts, k until end. [6 (7, 8, 9, 10) (11, 12, 13, 14, 15) sts rem]

Bind off rem 6 (7, 8, 9, 10) (11, 12, 13, 14, 15) sts. Break yarn, leaving a tail 2x the length of the shoulder for seaming.

## BACK

Rejoin yarn to RS of work.

**Row 1 (RS):** Bind off 4 (5, 5, 6, 6) (7, 7, 8, 8, 9) sts, k until end. [90 (101, 111, 122, 132) (143, 153, 164, 174, 185) sts rem]

**Row 2 (WS):** Bind off 4 (5, 5, 6, 6) (7, 7, 8, 8, 9) sts, p until end. [86 (96, 106, 116, 126) (136, 146, 156, 166, 176) sts rem]

**Row 3:** K1, ssk, k until last 3 sts, k2tog, k1. [84 (94, 104, 114, 124) (134, 144, 154, 164, 174) sts rem, 2 sts decreased]

**Row 4:** P all sts.

Repeat rows 3–4 a total of 5 (5, 6, 7, 7) (8, 9, 9, 10, 11) more times until 74 (84, 92, 100, 110) (118, 126, 136, 144, 152) sts rem.

**Next row (RS):** K all sts.

**Next row (WS):** P all sts.

Repeat last 2 rows until piece measures 16.75 (17.25, 17.75, 18.25, 18.75) (19.25, 19.75, 20.25, 20.75, 21.25)" / 43 (44, 45, 46, 48) (49, 50, 51, 53, 54) cm from the bottom of the folded hem.

**Next row (RS):** Bind off 5 (7, 8, 8, 9) (10, 11, 12, 13, 14) sts, k21 (24, 27, 30, 33) (36, 38, 42, 44, 46) *including the stitch on the right needle after the bind offs,* bind off 22 (22, 22, 24, 26) (26, 28, 28, 30, 32) sts, k until end.

Leave Back Right sts on a spare needle or scrap yarn to return to later.

## BACK LEFT
**Row 1 (WS):** Bind off 5 (7, 8, 8, 9) (10, 11, 12, 13, 14) sts, p until end. [21 (24, 27, 30, 33) (36, 38, 42, 44, 46) sts rem]

**Row 2:** K1, ssk, k until end. [20 (23, 26, 29, 32) (35, 37, 41, 43, 45) sts rem, 1 st decreased]

**Row 3:** Bind off 6 (7, 8, 9, 10) (11, 11, 13, 13, 14) sts, p until end. [14 (16, 18, 20, 22) (24, 26, 28, 30, 31) sts rem]

**Row 4:** K1, ssk, k until end. [13 (15, 17, 19, 21) (23, 25, 27, 29, 30) sts rem, 1 st decreased]

**Row 5:** Bind off 6 (7, 8, 9, 10) (11, 12, 13, 14, 14) sts, p until end. [7 (8, 9, 10, 11) (12, 13, 14, 15, 16) sts rem]

**Row 6:** K1, ssk, k until end. [6 (7, 8, 9, 10) (11, 12, 13, 14, 15) sts rem, 1 st decreased]

Bind off rem 6 (7, 8, 9, 10) (11, 12, 13, 14, 15) sts and break yarn.

## BACK RIGHT
Rejoin yarn to WS of work.

**Row 1 (WS):** P all sts.

**Row 2:** Bind off 6 (7, 8, 9, 10) (11, 11, 13, 13, 14) sts, k until last 3 sts, k2tog, k1. [14 (16, 18, 20, 22) (24, 26, 28, 30, 31) sts rem, 1 st decreased]

**Row 3:** P all sts.

**Row 4:** Bind off 6 (7, 8, 9, 10) (11, 11, 13, 13, 14) sts, k until last 3 sts, k2tog, k1. [7 (8, 9, 10, 11) (12, 13, 14, 15, 16) sts rem, 1 st decreased]

**Row 5:** P all sts.

**Row 6:** K until last 3 sts, k2tog, k1. [6 (7, 8, 9, 10) (11, 12, 13, 14, 15) sts rem, 1 st decreased]

Bind off rem 6 (7, 8, 9, 10) (11, 12, 13, 14, 15) sts and break yarn.

## Seaming the Shoulders

With the WS of the front and back pieces facing each other, use a tapestry needle and the horizontal invisible seaming technique to seam the shoulders using the tails from the front pieces.

## SLEEVES (MAKE 2)

Using US 6 (4 mm) needles and beginning with the center of the underarm, pick up and k4 (5, 5, 6, 6) (7, 7, 8, 8, 9) from the bind off sts, evenly pick up and k40 (40, 44, 46, 48) (52, 56, 60, 62, 62) towards the shoulder, pm, evenly pick up and k40 (40, 44, 46, 48) (52, 56, 60, 62, 62) back towards the underarm, and pick up and k4 (5, 5, 6, 6) (7, 7, 8, 8, 9) from the underarm bind off sts. Pm and join for working in the round. [88 (90, 98, 104, 108) (118, 126, 136, 140, 142) sts]

### Short Row Shaping

**Short row 1 (RS):** K until stm, sm, k4, turn.

**Short row 2 (WS):** MDS, p until stm, sm, p4, turn.

**Short row 3:** MDS, k until stm, sm, k until 4 sts past DS (resolving existing DS), turn.

**Short row 4:** MDS, p until stm, sm, p until 4 sts past DS (resolving existing DS), turn.

Repeat the last 2 rows 7 (7, 8, 9, 9) (10, 10, 11, 11, 11) more times. In your final row, after you turn your work, MDS, k until shoulder stm, remove marker, and continue in patt until BOR stm, resolving DS along the way. You will be working in the round for the remainder of the sleeve.

K all rounds, resolving the final DS along the way, until the sleeve measures 2 inches (5 cm) from the underarm edge, or until it reaches desired length.

Use a tapestry needle to insert a piece of scrap yarn in the last round worked.

Switch to US 4 (3.5 mm) needles.

**Next 4 rounds:** K all sts.

**Next round:** P all sts.

**Next 4 rounds:** K all sts.

Bind off very loosely. Break yarn and leave a tail 2x the circumference of the sleeve. Use the tail to whip stitch the bind off edge to the round with the scrap yarn. Remove scrap yarn.

## NECKBAND

Using US 6 (4 mm) needles and beginning with the right shoulder, evenly pick up and k the following sts: k4 down towards the back, k22 (22, 22, 24, 26) (26, 28, 28, 30, 32) from the back neck bind off sts, k4 up towards the left shoulder, k20 down toward the front, k10 (10, 10, 12, 14) (14, 16, 16, 18, 20) from the front neck bind off sts, then k20 towards the right shoulder. Pm and join for working in the round. [80 (80, 80, 84, 88) (88, 92, 92, 96, 100) sts]

**Rounds 2–6:** K all sts.

**Round 7:** P all sts.

**Rounds 8–12:** K all sts.

Bind off very loosely (using a larger needle can be helpful) and break yarn, leaving a tail 2x the circumference of the neckband. Use the tail to whip stitch the bind off edge to the pick up edge.

## POCKET FLAP

Position the project upside down to prepare for the pocket flap pickup (Image 9). Using US 6 (4 mm) needles, beginning with the st to the right of the pickup line, pick up and k18 (20, 20, 22, 22) (24, 24, 26, 28, 30). There will be 1 extra st on each side of the pocket (Images 10 & 11).

**Row 2 (WS):** P all sts.

**Row 3:** K all sts.

**Rows 4–7:** Repeat rows 2–3 (Image 12).

**Rows 8–10:** P all sts.

**Row 11:** K all sts.

**Row 12:** P all sts.

**Row 13:** K9 (10, 10, 11, 11) (12, 12, 13, 14, 15), place removable stm to mark the female side of the snap-on button, k9 (10, 10, 11, 11) (12, 12, 13, 14, 15).

**Row 14:** P all sts.

**Row 15:** K all sts.

**Row 16:** P all sts.

Bind off all sts and leave a tail 2.5x the width of the pocket flap.

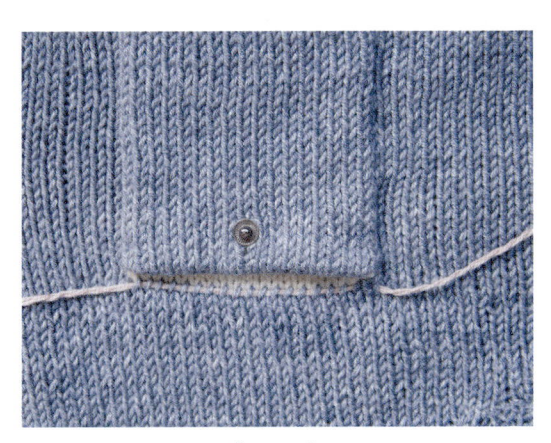

Image 9

Image 10: When picking up sts from the middle of the fabric, you will be inserting your right needle into the middle of the st.

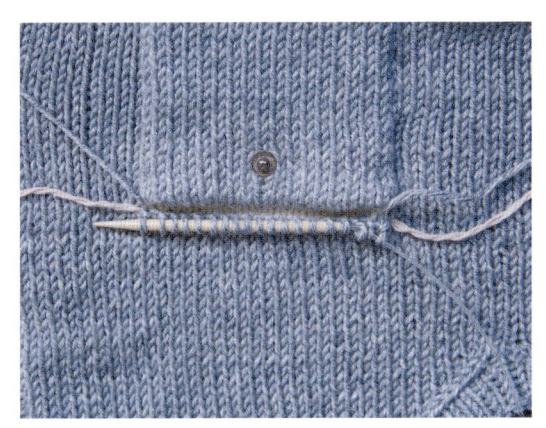

Image 11: After all sts are picked up, you will resume knitting as per the instructions.

Image 12: This is how the pocket flap should look like once rows 1–8 are knit.

Image 13

Image 14

## Install Snap-On Button

At this point, you will now install both sides of the snap-on button(s). It is possible to install them after the garment is completed, but it will be trickier due to the multiple layers of fabric. Be careful you are not trapping other parts of the garment in between the snap-on pieces. Note, the button is installed on the MC fabric only.

In the sample knit, the female side is installed on the WS of the pocket flap (facing down towards the exterior of the pocket), with the male side installed on the opposite end from the exterior pocket. Once placement is secured, remove both removable stms (Image 13).

Once the snap-on button sides are installed, fold the pocket flap so the purl round is now the bottom. Use a tapestry needle to whip stitch the bind off edge to the pick up edge (Image 14), and use the mattress st to seam the pocket flap edges to the tee (this will better secure the pocket flap in place).

## FINISHING

Turn the piece inside out. Measure a piece of MC yarn 2x the length of the seam edge of the pocket. Beginning from the top edge of one side of the pocket, use a tapestry needle to whip stitch the pocket lining to the WS of the garment down towards the bottom of the pocket, continue whip stitching across the bottom and then back up to the other side of the pocket. Make sure to go through both layers of the pocket lining. Weave in any loose ends and remove the CC yarn.

Block your project using your preferred method.

# Poppy Pocket Shorts

Knitting your own bottoms can be a daunting task for many knitters (myself included). Perhaps it's a relatively uncommon article of clothing to make, or it can be perceived as a fairly time-consuming project. Fortunately, my fear was largely unfounded. If you have had or have these thoughts, fear no more. You *can* and *should* knit your own shorts!

The Poppy Pocket Shorts are cargo-style shorts that are the matching companion piece to the Poppy Pocket Tee (page 53). These high-waisted shorts have an A-line silhouette that gives ample room for the thighs while also providing a flattering fit for your waist and butt. The roomy side pockets are an aesthetic detail but also give you an extra place to place small items while on the go. The drawstring will ensure a flexible and comfortable fit. Whether worn as a lounge set at home or out and about, be prepared to be frequently asked, "You made that?" Yes. Yes, I did.

## Construction Notes

*The shorts are worked in the round from the top down, beginning with a folded hem that includes drawstring holes at the waistband. German short rows are worked to add additional length to the back of the shorts. Increases are then worked on the inner pant legs until the final hip circumference is reached. The legs are then separated and worked in the round, finished with a folded hem. Pockets are knit separately and seamed to the shorts, and the pocket flaps are picked up from the shorts and knit flat. Finally, an I-cord is worked to create the drawstring for the shorts.*

## SKILL LEVEL
*Intermediate*

## SIZING
*XS (S, M, L, XL) (2XL, 3XL, 4XL, 5XL, 6XL)*

*Waist circumference of 24.75 (26.25, 29, 33.5, 36.25) (40.75, 45, 46.5, 49.5, 52.25)" / 63 (67, 74, 85, 93) (104, 115, 119, 126, 134) cm, blocked*

## Materials

### Yarn
*DK weight, Debbie Bliss Cotton Denim DK in color 02 (100% cotton), 218 yds (200 m) per 100-g skein*

*An alternate sample was also knit with We Are Knitters The Cotton in Canyon Rose.*

*Any DK or worsted weight yarn can be used for this pattern as long as it matches gauge.*

### Yardage/Meterage
*680 (710, 795, 910, 1040) (1105, 1215, 1265, 1280, 1420) yds / 620 (650, 725, 830, 950) (1010, 1110, 1155, 1170, 1300) m of DK or worsted weight yarn*

### Needles

**For waistband:** *US 4 (3.5 mm), 24- to 60-inch (60- to 150-cm) circular needles*

**For shorts:** *US 6 (4 mm), 24- to 60-inch (60- to 150-cm) circular needles*

**For drawstring:** *US 4 (3.5 mm) straight or double pointed needles*

### Notions

*Removable stitch markers*

*Safety pin*

*Scrap yarn in a contrasting color*

*2 sets of snap-on buttons (8–12 mm, optional)*

*Stitch markers*

*Tapestry needle*

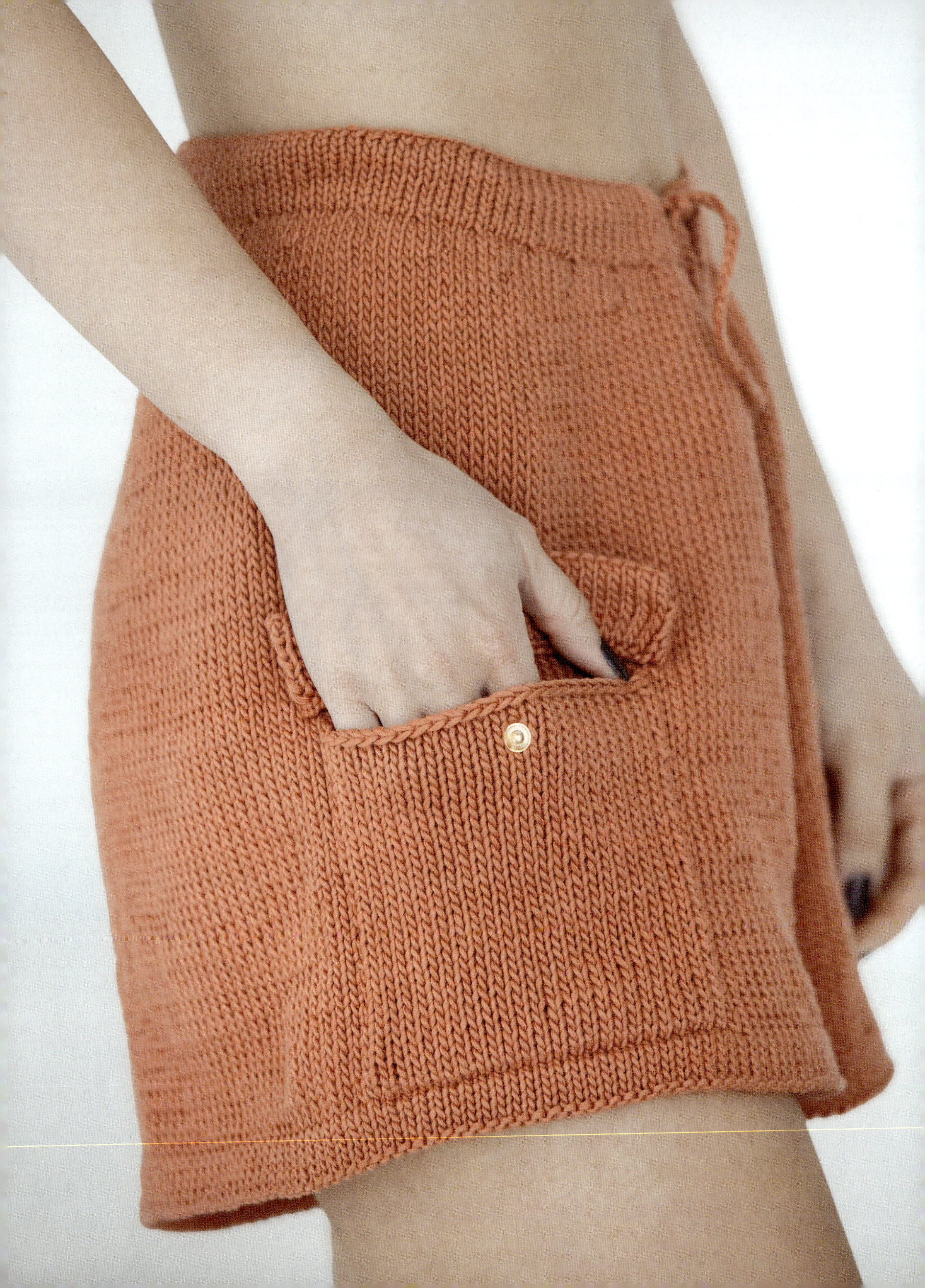

## GAUGE

*22 sts x 27 rows = 4 inches (10 cm) in stockinette st using larger needles (blocked)*

## TECHNIQUES

*Backwards Loop Cast On (page 142)*

*German Short Rows (page 151)*

*Horizontal Invisible Seam (page 149)*

*I-Cord (page 153)*

*Mattress Stitch (page 150)*

*Whip Stitch (page 150)*

# ABBREVIATIONS

| | |
|---|---|
| BOR | beginning of round |
| CSD | centered single decrease: slip 2 sts knitwise (one after another); insert the left needle into the front of both slipped stitches, knit together; insert the left needle into the second of the just decreased stitches, placing it onto the left needle, ready to be worked; insert the right needle into the next 2 sts to k2tog [1 st decreased] |
| DS | double stitch |
| k | knit |
| m1l | make 1 left: use the left needle to pick up the strand between the last worked st and the next unworked st from front to back, knit this st through the back loop [1 st increased] |
| m1r | make 1 right: use the left needle to pick up the strand between the last worked st and the next unworked st from back to front, knit this st through the front loop [1 st increased] |
| MBM | middle back marker |
| MDS | make double stitch [see German short rows in Techniques] |
| p | purl |
| patt | pattern |
| pm | place marker |
| rep | repeat |
| sm | slip marker |
| st(s) | stitch(es) |
| stm(s) | stitch marker(s) |
| yo | yarnover |

## SIZING CHART

| | XS | S | M | L | XL | 2XL | 3XL | 4XL | 5XL | 6XL | |
|---|---|---|---|---|---|---|---|---|---|---|---|
| A) Waist Circumference | 24.75 | 26.25 | 29 | 33.5 | 37.75 | 40.75 | 45 | 46.5 | 49.5 | 52.25 | in |
| | 63 | 67 | 74 | 85 | 97 | 104 | 115 | 119 | 126 | 134 | cm |
| B) Hip Circumference | 49.75 | 51.75 | 55.25 | 61.5 | 67 | 71.25 | 76.75 | 78.5 | 82.25 | 86.5 | in |
| | 127 | 132 | 141 | 157 | 170 | 182 | 195 | 200 | 209 | 220 | cm |
| C) Crotch Depth | 7.75 | 7.75 | 7.75 | 8 | 8 | 8.25 | 8.25 | 8.25 | 8.25 | 8.5 | in |
| | 20 | 20 | 20 | 21 | 21 | 22 | 22 | 22 | 22 | 22 | cm |
| D) Thigh Circumference | 26.75 | 27.75 | 29.75 | 33 | 36 | 38.5 | 41.25 | 42.25 | 44.25 | 46.5 | in |
| | 68 | 71 | 76 | 84 | 92 | 98 | 105 | 108 | 113 | 119 | cm |
| E) Inseam from Crotch to Hem | 3.5 | 3.5 | 4 | 4 | 4.5 | 4.5 | 5 | 5 | 5.5 | 5.5 | in |
| | 9 | 9 | 11 | 11 | 12 | 12 | 13 | 13 | 14 | 14 | cm |
| F) Full Shorts Length | 14.75 | 14.75 | 15.5 | 15.75 | 16.25 | 17 | 17.5 | 17.75 | 18.25 | 18.75 | in |
| | 38 | 38 | 40 | 41 | 42 | 44 | 45 | 46 | 47 | 48 | cm |
| G) Pocket Width | 4.75 | 4.75 | 5 | 5.5 | 5.75 | 6.5 | 7 | 7.25 | 7.75 | 8 | in |
| | 13 | 13 | 13 | 14 | 15 | 17 | 18 | 19 | 20 | 21 | cm |
| H) Pocket Depth | 5 | 5 | 5.5 | 5.75 | 6 | 7 | 7.5 | 7.5 | 8 | 8.5 | in |
| | 13 | 13 | 14 | 15 | 16 | 18 | 20 | 20 | 21 | 22 | cm |

The shorts are designed with -2 to 1.5 inches (-5 to 4 cm) of ease at the waist. Select the size that is closest to your waist measurement, as the hips and thighs have an abundant amount of positive ease. Sample shown is knit in size XS with neutral ease.

## SCHEMATIC

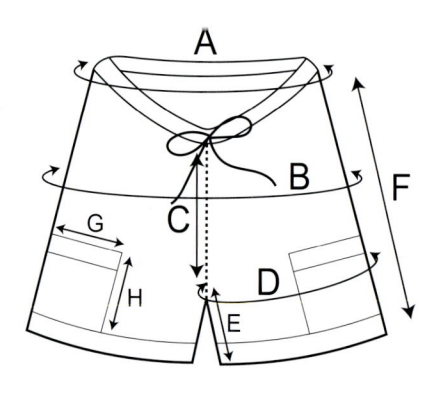

Light & Breezy Knitwear

# POPPY POCKET SHORTS PATTERN

## TOP HEM
Using US 4 (3.5 mm) needles, cast on 136 (144, 160, 184, 208) (224, 248, 256, 272, 288) sts using the longtail cast on method. Pm and join for working in the round.

**Rounds 1–8:** K all sts.

**Round 9:** P all sts.

**Rounds 10–13:** K all sts.

**Round 14:** K4, yo, CSD, k until last 7 sts, CSD, yo, k4.

**Rounds 15–18:** K all sts.

## Create Folded Hem
Fold your work so the purl round is now the bottom. Pick up the corresponding st from the cast on edge and place on left needle. K it together with the st from the current round. Repeat until you reach the final st.

**Increase round:** (K4, m1r) 17 (18, 20, 23, 26) (28, 31, 32, 34, 36) times, pm for middle back (MBM), *k4, m1r; rep from * until end. [170 (180, 200, 230, 260) (280, 310, 320, 340, 360) sts]

Switch to US 6 (4 mm) needles.

## Rear Shaping
**Row 1 (RS):** K until MBM, sm, k6, turn.

**Row 2 (WS):** MDS, p until MBM, sm, p6, turn.

**Row 3:** MDS, k until MBM, sm, k until 6 sts past DS, turn.

**Row 4:** MDS, p until MBM, sm, p until 6 sts past DS, turn.

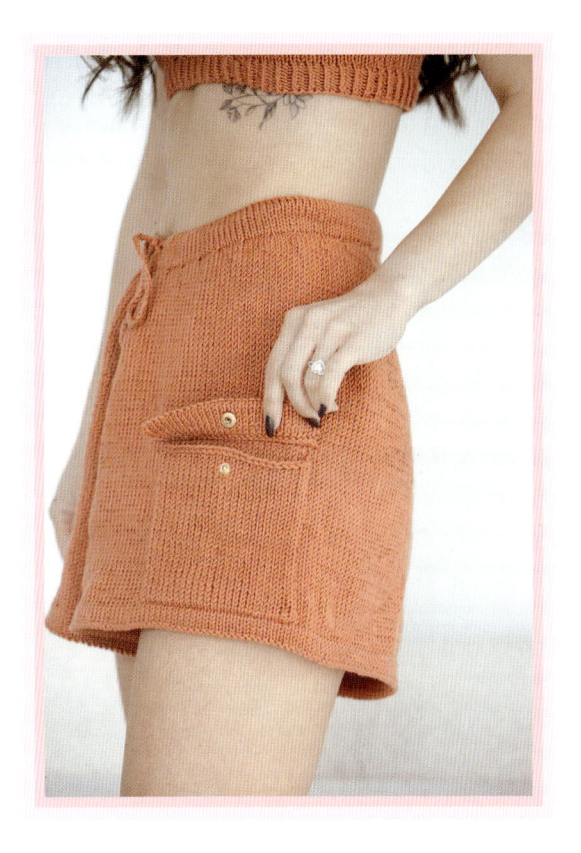

Repeat rows 3–4 a total of 10 (10, 11, 11, 11) (12, 12, 13, 13, 14) more times. In your final row, after you turn your work, MDS, k until MBM, sm, and continue in patt until BOR stm, resolving DS along the way. You will resolve the final DS during the next round.

**Increase round:** K1, m1l, k until 1 st before MBM, m1r, k1, sm, k1, m1l, k until 1 st before BOR stm, m1r, k1. [174 (184, 204, 234, 264) (284, 314, 324, 344, 364), 4 sts increased]

**Next round:** K all sts.

Repeat last 2 rounds a total of 25 (25, 25, 26, 26) (27, 27, 27, 27, 28) more times until you have 274 (284, 304, 338, 368) (392, 422, 432, 452, 476) sts.

K all rounds until left leg measures 2.5 (2.5, 3, 3, 3.5) (3.5, 4, 4, 4.5, 4.5)" / 7 (7, 8, 8, 9) (9, 11, 11, 12, 12) cm from the set-up round, or until desired length.

**NOTE:** *There will be an additional 1 inch (3 cm) of length added after this point for the hem.*

*Place Marker for Pockets*
**Next round:** K73 (76, 82, 90, 99) (106, 113, 116, 122, 128), place removable stm to mark left edge of right leg pocket, k26 (26, 28, 30, 32) (36, 38, 40, 42, 44), place removable stm to mark right edge of right leg pocket, k until end.

**NOTE:** *The removable stm is placed in between sts.*

Insert a piece of scrap yarn in a contrasting color in the last round worked.

Switch to US 4 (3.5 mm) needles.

**Next 5 rounds:** K all sts.

**Next round:** P all sts.

**Next 5 rounds:** K all sts.

Bind off all sts very loosely and leave a tail 2.5x the circumference of the leg. Use a tapestry needle to whip stitch the bind off edge to the round indicated by the scrap yarn. Remove scrap yarn.

## Separate the Legs
### RIGHT LEG
**Set-up round:** Remove BOR stm and transfer the next 137 (142, 152, 169, 184) (196, 211, 216, 226, 238) sts for the left leg to a holder or spare yarn to return to later, removing the MBM in the process. Using the backwards loop method, cast on 5 (5, 6, 6, 7) (8, 8, 8, 9, 9) sts, pm for new BOR, cast on 5 (5, 6, 6, 7) (8, 8, 8, 9, 9) sts, k137 (142, 152, 169, 184) (196, 211, 216, 226, 238) from the remaining sts to create the right leg. [147 (152, 164, 181, 198) (212, 227, 232, 244, 256) sts]

## LEFT LEG

Move live sts to needles and rejoin yarn to beginning of round.

**Set-up round:** K137 (142, 152, 169, 184) (196, 211, 216, 226, 238) from the live sts, pick up and k5 (5, 6, 6, 7) (8, 8, 8, 9, 9) from the crotch cast on sts from the right leg, pm for new BOR, pick up and k5 (5, 6, 6, 7) (8, 8, 8, 9, 9) from remaining crotch cast on sts from the right leg. [147 (152, 164, 181, 198) (212, 227, 232, 244, 256) sts]

K all rounds until right leg measures 2.5 (2.5, 3, 3, 3.5) (3.5, 4, 4, 4.5, 4.5)" / 7 (7, 8, 8, 9) (9, 11, 11, 12, 12) cm from the set-up round, or until desired length to match the right leg.

*Place Marker for Pockets*
**Next round:** K48 (50, 54, 61, 67) (70, 76, 76, 80, 84), place removable stm to mark left edge of left leg pocket, k26 (26, 28, 30, 32) (36, 38, 40, 42, 44), place removable stm to mark right edge of left leg pocket, k until end.

Switch to US 4 (3.5 mm) needles.

Insert a piece of scrap yarn in a contrasting color in the last round worked.

**Next 5 rounds:** K all sts.

**Next round:** P all sts.

**Next 5 rounds:** K all sts.

Bind off all sts very loosely and leave a tail 2.5x the circumference of the leg. Use a tapestry needle to whip stitch the bind off edge to the round indicated by the scrap yarn. Remove scrap yarn.

## POCKETS (MAKE 2)

**NOTE:** *If you leave a long enough tail before cast on and after bind off, you will have enough yarn for seaming.*

Using US 6 (4 mm) needles, cast on 26 (26, 28, 30, 32) (36, 38, 40, 42, 44) sts using the longtail cast on method.

**Next row (WS):** P all sts.

**Next row (RS):** K all sts.

Repeat last 2 rows until pocket measures 5 (5, 5.5, 5.75, 6) (7, 7.5, 7.5, 8, 8.5)" / 13 (13, 14, 15, 16) (18, 20, 20, 21, 22) cm.

Bind off tightly and break yarn, leaving a tail 2.5x the length of the pocket for seaming the right edge of the pocket to the shorts. Use a removable stm to mark the placement of the male side of the snap-on button. I suggest placing the snap-on button 4 rows below the bind off edge in the middle of the pocket. Install the snap-on button and remove stm.

### Seam the Pockets

Beginning with one leg, position the pocket so the cast on edge sits between the removable stms. Use pins to assist you if necessary. Beginning with the top right edge, use a tapestry needle and the mattress st to seam the pocket to the leg. Once you reach the cast on edge of the pocket, use the horizontal invisible seam to seam the bottom edge. Finally, use the mattress st to seam the left edge of the pocket to the leg. Do not weave in any loose ends yet, as you might be able to use the remaining tail(s) to seam the sides of the pocket flap.

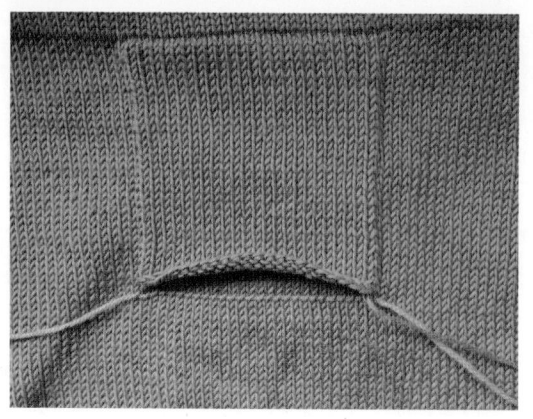

Image 1

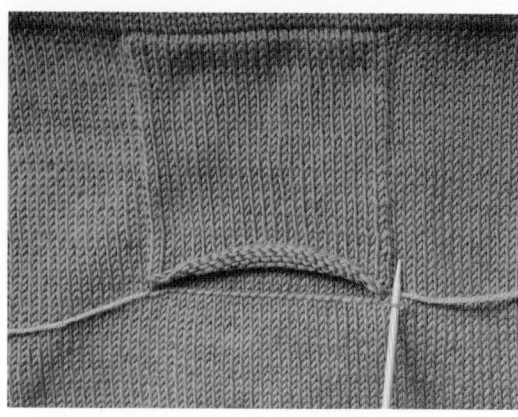

Image 2: When picking up sts from the middle of the fabric, you will be inserting your right needle into the middle of the st.

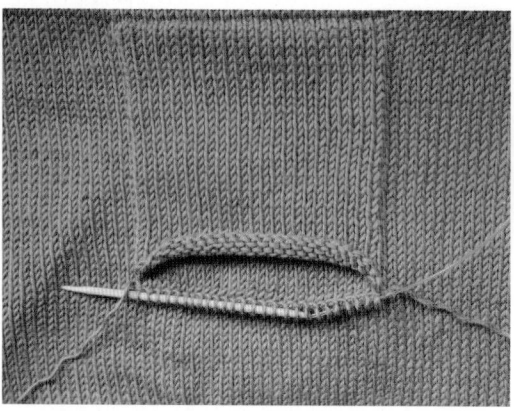

Image 3: After all sts are picked up, you will resume knitting as per the instructions.

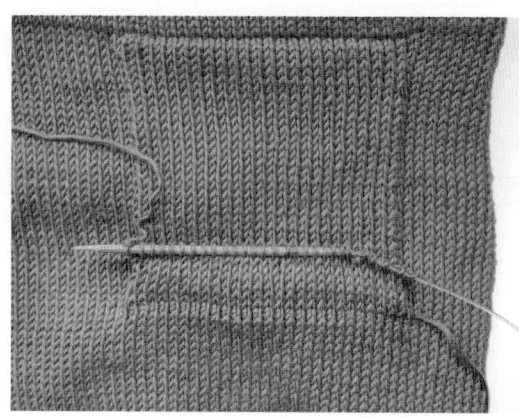

Image 4: This is how the pocket flap should look once rows 1–8 are knit.

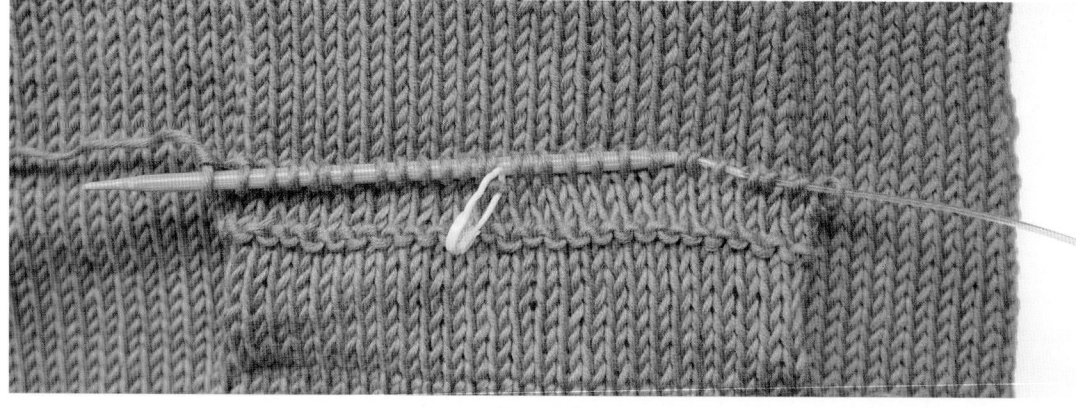

Image 5

72　　Light & Breezy Knitwear

Image 6

Image 7

## POCKET FLAP (MAKE 2)
Position the project upside down to prepare for the pocket flap pickup (Image 1). Feel free to use a piece of contrasting yarn to mark the row. Using US 6 (4 mm) needles, beginning with the st to the right of the pickup line, pick up and k28 (28, 30, 32, 34) (38, 40, 42, 44, 46). There will be one extra st on each side of the pocket (Images 2 & 3).

**Row 2 (WS):** P all sts.

**Row 3:** K all sts.

**Rows 4–7:** Repeat rows 2–3 (Image 4).

**Rows 8–10:** P all sts.

**Row 11:** K all sts.

**Row 12:** P all sts.

**Row 13:** K14 (14, 15, 16, 17) (19, 20, 21, 22, 23), place removable stm to mark the female side of the snap-on button, k14 (14, 15, 16, 17) (19, 20, 21, 22, 23) (Image 5).

**Row 14:** P all sts.

**Row 15:** K all sts.

**Row 16:** P all sts.

Bind off all sts and leave a tail 2.5x the width of the pocket flap.

### Pocket Flap Finishing
Install the female side of the snap-on button (Image 6). Once installed, fold the pocket flap so the purl round is now the bottom. Use a tapestry needle to whip stitch the bind off edge to the pick up edge (Image 7), and use the mattress st to seam the pocket flap edges to the shorts (this will better secure the pocket flap in place).

### I-Cord Drawstring
Using US 4 (3.5 mm) needles, cast on 2 sts using the longtail method. Slide sts to end of needle (or transfer back to left needle).

**Next row:** K2. Slide sts to end of needle (or transfer back to left needle).

Repeat last row until drawstring measures 35 (37, 40, 44, 48) (52, 56, 58, 61, 63)" / 89 (94, 102, 112, 122) (133, 143, 148, 155, 161) cm or until desired length. Bind off.

## FINISHING
Secure a safety pin to one end of your cord and feed it into one of the openings of your waistband until it comes out the other opening. Weave in any remaining loose ends. Block your project using your preferred method.

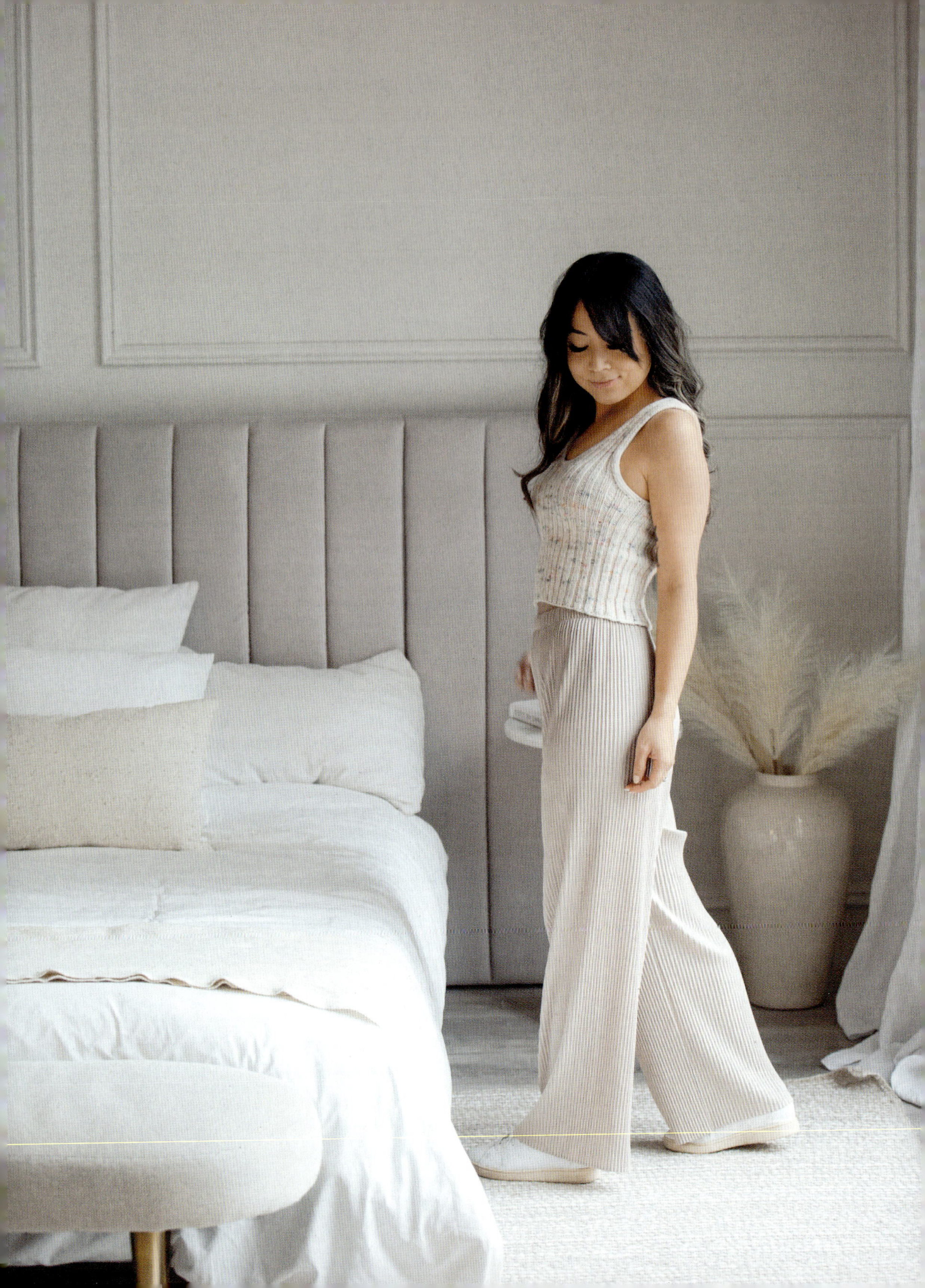

# Wisteria Tank

A classic ribbed tank is a wardrobe essential. Slightly cropped with a crew neck, the Wisteria Tank is a simple top that will add refinement and style to any outfit. The 2x2 ribbing creates a form-fitting and elegant silhouette that is comfortable to wear and flattering for all body types. The ribbing also makes the project a quick knit and the I-cord edge adds a polished finish to the garment. The simplicity of the design allows for easy outfit coordination—this tank will look good with *everything*. Whether you wear it on its own or layered with another top, the Wisteria Tank will help you create an effortlessly chic outfit.

## Construction Notes

The tank is worked in the round from the bottom up in 2x2 ribbing before separating for the front and back pieces. The remainder of the body is worked flat until the armhole shaping is completed and the correct length is achieved. Once the front and back pieces are completed, the shoulders are seamed. Finally, an I-cord edge is worked around the neckline and both armhole edges for a clean finish.

## SKILL LEVEL
Advanced Beginner

## SIZING
XS (S, M, L, XL) (2XL, 3XL, 4XL, 5XL, 6XL)

Circumference at the widest part of bust 28.75 (32, 36.75, 40, 44.75) (48, 52.75, 56, 60.75, 64)" / 73 (81, 94, 102, 114) (122, 134, 142, 155, 163) cm, blocked

## Materials

### Yarn
DK weight, Koigu Jasmine in J132S (100% wool), 242 yds (221 m) per 100-g skein

Any DK weight yarn can be used for this pattern as long as it matches gauge.

### Yardage/Meterage
330 (365, 420, 490, 520) (560, 630, 665, 735, 770) yds / 300 (335, 385, 450, 475) (510, 575, 610, 670, 705) m of DK weight yarn

### Needles
**For body:** US 6 (4 mm), 24- to 60-inch (60- to 150-cm) circular needle

**For armhole and neckline edge:** US 4 (3.5 mm) double pointed needles

### Notions
Removable stitch marker(s)

Stitch marker

Tapestry needle

## GAUGE
20 sts x 28 rounds = 4 inches (10 cm) in 2x2 ribbing using larger needles (blocked and stretched)

**NOTE:** *It is difficult to measure gauge accurately when it comes to ribbing due to the amount of stretch. If you are able to get close to gauge stretched OR unstretched, the garment will fit.*

## TECHNIQUES
Horizontal Invisible Seam (page 149)

Kitchener Stitch (page 147)

Provisional Cast On (page 145)

# ABBREVIATIONS

| | |
|---|---|
| 0 or - | no stitch / step does not apply to your size |
| BOR | beginning of round |
| DPN(s) | double pointed needles |
| k | knit |
| k2tog | knit 2 sts together [1 st decreased] |
| p | purl |
| patt | pattern |
| pm | place marker |
| rem | remain(ing) |
| rep | repeat |
| RS | right side |
| ssk | slip 2 sts knitwise, one at a time; move both stitches back to the left needle; knit these 2 sts together through the back loops [1 st decreased] |
| st(s) | stitch(es) |
| stm(s) | stitch marker(s) |
| work(ing) even | continue working the pattern as established without any increases or decreases |
| WS | wrong side |

## SIZING CHART

|  | XS | S | M | L | XL | 2XL | 3XL | 4XL | 5XL | 6XL |  |
|---|---|---|---|---|---|---|---|---|---|---|---|
| A) Body Circumference | 28.75 | 32 | 36.75 | 40 | 44.75 | 48 | 52.75 | 56 | 60.75 | 64 | in |
|  | 73 | 81 | 94 | 102 | 114 | 122 | 134 | 142 | 155 | 163 | cm |
| B) Armhole Depth | 7.5 | 8 | 8.5 | 9 | 9.5 | 10 | 10.5 | 11 | 11.5 | 12 | in |
|  | 19 | 20 | 22 | 23 | 24 | 26 | 27 | 28 | 29 | 31 | cm |
| C) Garment Length | 16.5 | 17 | 17.5 | 18 | 18.5 | 19 | 19.5 | 20 | 20.5 | 21 | in |
|  | 42 | 43 | 45 | 46 | 47 | 48 | 50 | 51 | 52 | 53 | cm |

The top is designed with -2 to 1 inches (-5 to 3 cm) of negative to positive ease. Sample shown is knit in size S. If in between sizes, it is recommended to select the smaller size.

## SCHEMATIC

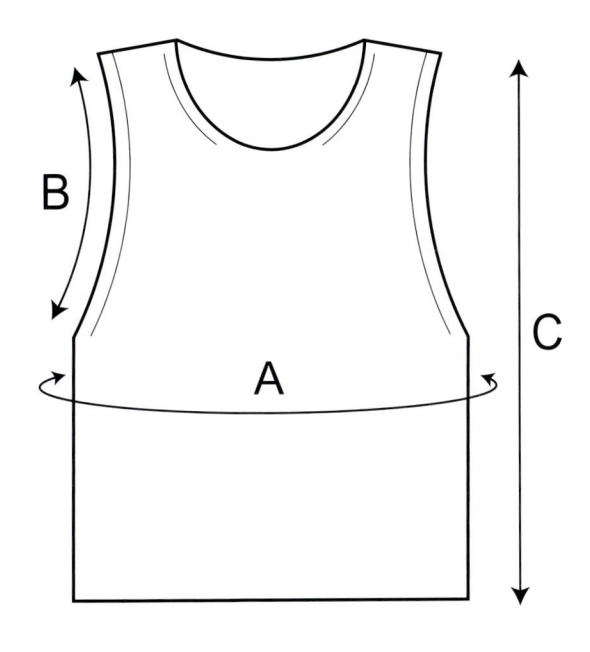

Knit + Athleisure = Knitleisure

# WISTERIA TANK PATTERN

## BODY

Using US 6 (4 mm) needles, cast on 144 (160, 184, 200, 224) (240, 264, 280, 304, 320) sts using the longtail cast on method. Pm and join for working in the round.

**Set-up round:** P1, *k2, p2; rep from * until last 3 sts, k2, p1.

Repeat last round until your piece measures 9 inches (23 cm).

Separate for Front/Back.

## BACK

**Row 1 (RS):** Remove BOR marker. Bind off 4 (4, 4, 6, 6) (8, 8, 8, 10, 10) sts, work in patt for 68 (76, 88, 94, 106) (112, 124, 132, 142, 150) sts. Leave rem 72 (80, 92, 100, 112) (120, 132, 140, 152, 160) front sts on a holder or spare yarn to return to later. [68 (76, 88, 94, 106) (112, 124, 132, 142, 150) sts rem]

**Row 2 (WS):** Bind off 4 (4, 4, 6, 6) (8, 8, 8, 10, 10) sts, work in patt until end. [64 (72, 84, 88, 100) (104, 116, 124, 132, 140) sts rem]

**Row 3:** K2, ssk, work in patt until last 4 sts, k2tog, k2. [62 (70, 82, 86, 98) (102, 114, 122, 130, 138) sts rem, 2 sts decreased]

**Row 4:** Work in patt.

Repeat rows 3–4 a total of 3 (3, 3, 3, 5) (5, 5, 7, 7, 7) more times until 56 (64, 76, 80, 88) (92, 104, 108, 116, 124) sts rem.

> **NOTE:** *There is an additional knit stitch on each outer edge intended for sleeve pickup.*

**Row 1 (RS):** K2, ssk, work in patt until last 4 sts, k2tog, k2. [54 (62, 74, 78, 86) (90, 102, 106, 114, 122) sts rem, 2 sts decreased]

**Rows 2–4:** Work in patt.

Repeat rows 1–4 a total of 3 more times until 48 (56, 68, 72, 80) (84, 96, 100, 108, 116) sts rem.

Work even until piece measures 15.5 (16, 16.5, 17, 17.5) (18, 18.5, 19, 19.5, 20)" / 39 (41, 42, 43, 44) (46, 47, 48, 50, 51) cm, ending on a WS row.

**Next row (RS):** Work 15 (15, 19, 19, 23) (23, 27, 27, 27, 31) sts in patt, bind off 18 (26, 30, 34, 34) (38, 42, 46, 54, 54) sts, work rem 15 (15, 19, 19, 23) (23, 27, 27, 27, 31) sts in patt.

Leave Back Right sts on a spare needle or scrap yarn to return to later.

## BACK LEFT

**Row 1 (WS):** Work in patt.

**Row 2 (RS):** K1, ssk, work in patt until end. [14 (14, 18, 18, 22) (22, 26, 26, 26, 30) sts rem, 1 st decreased]

**Row 3:** Work in patt.

Repeat rows 2–3 a total of 2 more times until 12 (12, 16, 16, 20) (20, 24, 24, 24, 28) sts rem. Bind off all sts.

## BACK RIGHT

Rejoin yarn to WS of work.

**Row 1 (WS):** Work in patt.

**Row 2 (RS):** Work in patt until last 3 sts, k2tog, k1. [14 (14, 18, 18, 22) (22, 26, 26, 26, 30) sts rem, 1 st decreased]

**Row 3:** Work in patt.

Repeat rows 2–3 a total of 2 more times until 12 (12, 16, 16, 20) (20, 24, 24, 24, 28) sts rem. Bind off all sts.

## FRONT
Rejoin yarn to RS of work.

**Row 1 (RS):** Bind off 4 (4, 4, 6, 6) (8, 8, 8, 10, 10) sts, work in patt until end. [68 (76, 88, 94, 106) (112, 124, 132, 142, 150) sts rem]

**Row 2 (WS):** Bind off 4 (4, 4, 6, 6) (8, 8, 8, 10, 10) sts, work in patt until end. [64 (72, 84, 88, 100) (104, 116, 124, 132, 140) sts rem]

**Row 3:** K2, ssk, work in patt until last 4 sts, k2tog, k2. [62 (70, 82, 86, 98) (102, 114, 122, 130, 138) sts rem, 2 sts decreased]

**Row 4:** Work in patt.

Repeat rows 3–4 a total of 3 (3, 3, 3, 5) (5, 5, 7, 7, 7) more times until 56 (64, 76, 80, 88) (92, 104, 108, 116, 124) sts rem.

### Separate for Front Left/Right
**Next row (RS):** K2, ssk, work 19 (23, 27, 29, 33) (35, 39, 41, 43, 47) sts in patt, bind off 10 (10, 14, 14, 14) (14, 18, 18, 22, 22) sts, work in patt until last 4 sts, k2tog, k2. You will now have 22 (26, 30, 32, 36) (38, 42, 44, 46, 50) sts on each side of the bindoffs. Turn work and leave rem front left sts on a holder or spare yarn to return to later.

## FRONT RIGHT
**Rows 1–3:** Work in patt.

**Row 4 (RS):** K2, ssk, work in patt until last 4 sts, k2tog, k2. [20 (24, 28, 30, 34) (36, 40, 42, 44, 48) sts rem, 2 sts decreased]

Repeat rows 1–4 a total of 2 more times until 16 (20, 24, 26, 30) (32, 36, 38, 40, 44) sts rem.

### Neck Decreases Only
**Rows 1–3:** Work in patt.

**Row 4 (RS):** K2, ssk, work in patt until end. [15 (19, 23, 25, 29) (31, 35, 37, 39, 43) sts rem, 1 st decreased]

Repeat rows 1–4 a total of 3 (6, 5, 6, 6) (7, 5, 6, 6, 6) more times until 12 (13, 18, 19, 23) (24, 30, 31, 33, 37) sts rem.

*Sizes S–6XL only*
Repeat rows 3–4 a total of - (1, 2, 3, 3) (4, 6, 7, 9, 9) more time(s) until - (12, 16, 16, 20) (20, 24, 24, 24, 28) sts rem.

*All sizes resume*
Work even until piece measures 16.5 (17, 17.5, 18, 18.5) (19, 19.5, 20, 20.5, 21)" / 42 (43, 44, 46, 47) (48, 50, 51, 52, 53) cm, ending on a WS row. Bind off all sts.

Knit + Athleisure = Knitleisure        79

## FRONT LEFT

Rejoin yarn to WS of work.

**Rows 1–3:** Work in patt.

**Row 4 (RS):** K2, ssk, work in patt until last 4 sts, k2tog, k2. [20 (24, 28, 30, 34) (36, 40, 42, 44, 48) sts rem, 2 sts decreased]

Repeat rows 1–4 a total of 2 more times until 16 (20, 24, 26, 30) (32, 36, 38, 40, 44) sts rem.

### Neck Decreases Only

**Rows 1–3:** Work in patt.

**Row 4 (RS):** Work in patt until last 4 sts, k2tog, k2. [15 (19, 23, 25, 29) (31, 35, 37, 39, 43) sts rem, 1 st decreased]

Repeat rows 1–4 a total of 3 (6, 5, 6, 6) (7, 5, 6, 6, 6) more times until 12 (13, 18, 19, 23) (24, 30, 31, 33, 37) sts rem.

*Sizes S–6XL only*
Repeat rows 3–4 a total of - (1, 2, 3, 3) (4, 6, 7, 9, 9) more time(s) until - (12, 16, 16, 20) (20, 24, 24, 24, 28) sts rem.

*All sizes resume*
Work even until piece measures 16.5 (17, 17.5, 18, 18.5) (19, 19.5, 20, 20.5, 21)" / 42 (43, 44, 46, 47) (48, 50, 51, 52, 53) cm, ending on a WS row. Bind off all sts.

### Seaming the Shoulders

With the WS of the front and back pieces facing each other, use a tapestry needle and the horizontal invisible seaming technique to seam the shoulders.

## APPLIED I-CORD ARMHOLE EDGE (MAKE 2)

Using US 4 (3.5 mm) DPNs and your preferred provisional cast on method, cast on 3 sts. Do not turn. From the RS of the garment and beginning at the bottom center of the armhole edge, pick up and bind off the armhole sts as described below using the following applied I cord edge technique:

1. Pick up and knit the next stitch in the armhole edge. [4 sts]
2. Slide the sts to the other end of the needle.
3. Bring the working yarn across the back of the sts. K2, ssk. [3 sts rem, 1 st decreased]

Continue picking up and binding off 1 st per bind off edge, and then 1 st per row up towards the shoulder and back down towards the beginning of the I-cord.

Break the yarn, leaving a 6-inch (15-cm) tail. Move provisional cast on sts to one needle and close the ends of the I-cord together using the Kitchener stitch.

## APPLIED I-CORD NECKLINE
Using US 4 (3.5 mm) DPNs and your preferred provisional cast on method, cast on 3 sts. Do not turn. From the RS of the garment and beginning at the left shoulder, pick up and bind off the neckline sts as described below using the following applied I-cord edge technique:

1. Pick up and knit the next stitch in the neckline. [4 sts]
2. Slide the sts to the other end of the needle.
3. Bring the working yarn across the back of the sts. K2, ssk. [3 sts rem, 1 st decreased]

Continue picking up and binding off 1 st per row and 1 st per bind off edge, down towards the center front, up towards the right shoulder, then across the back neck sts until you reach the left shoulder.

Break the yarn, leaving a 6-inch (15-cm) tail. Move provisional cast on sts to one needle and close the ends of the I-cord together using the Kitchener stitch.

## FINISHING
Weave in any loose ends. Block your project using your preferred method.

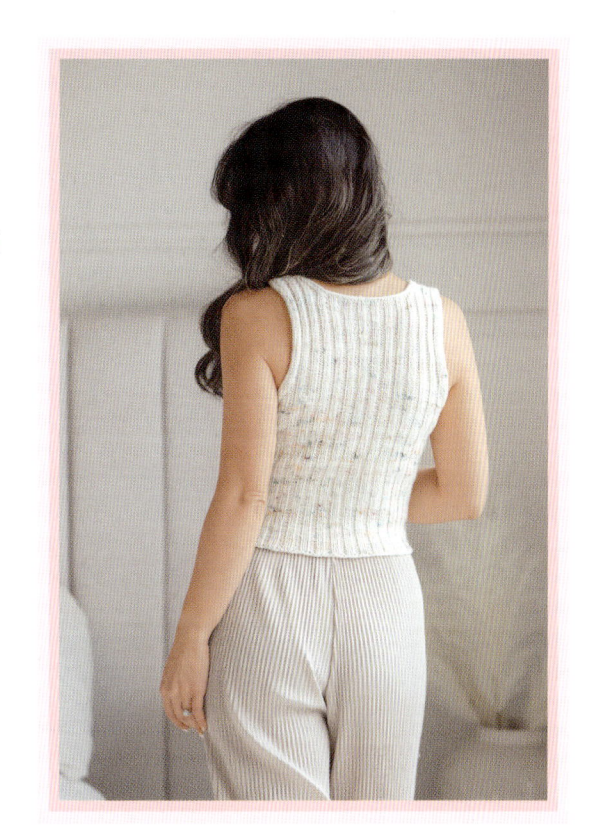

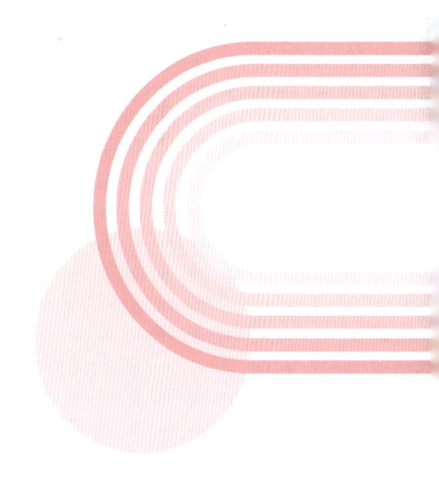

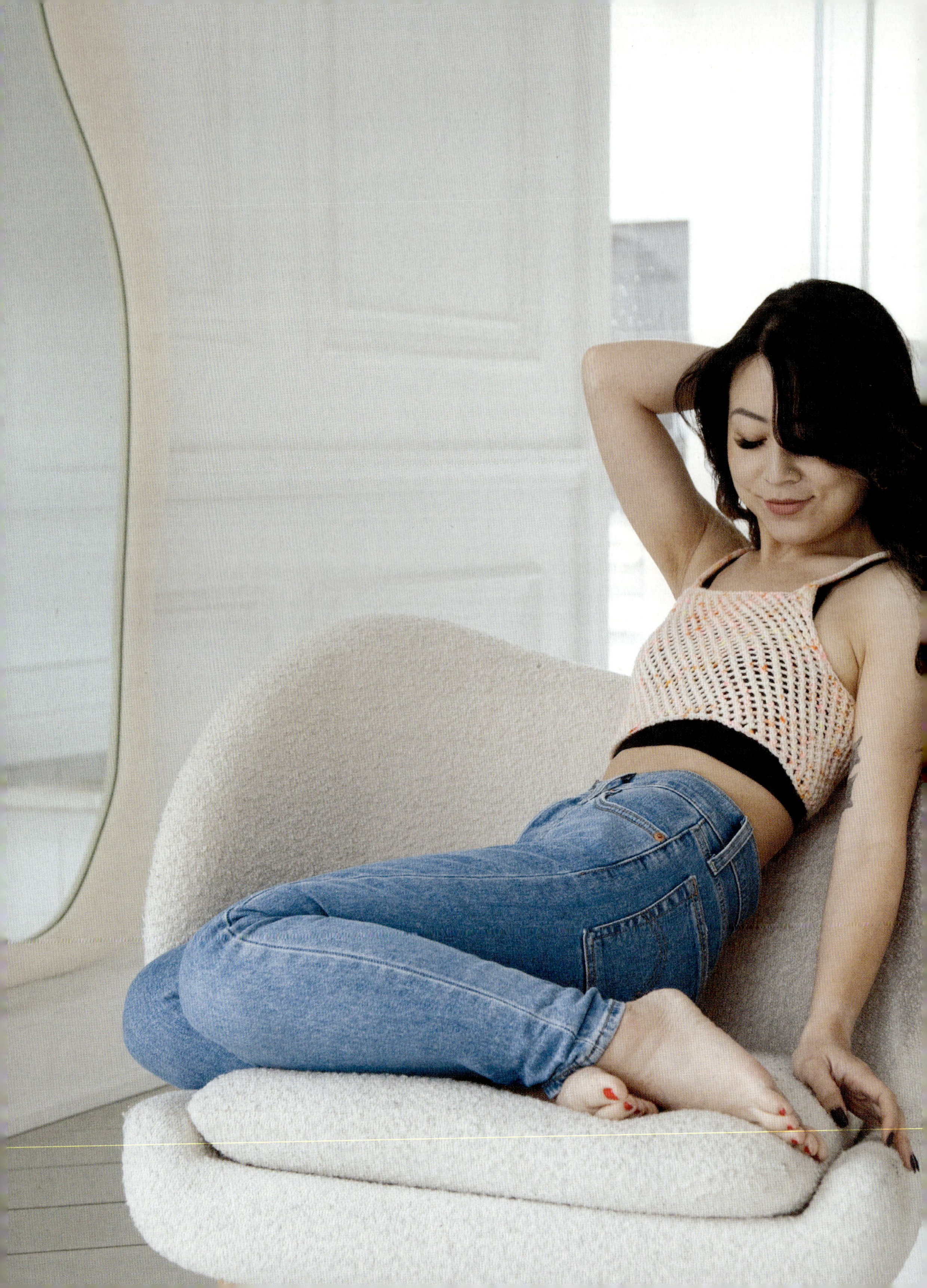

# Festival & Beach Knits

## Garments to Wear Under the Sun or in the Sand

Until recent years, "skimpy" and "sexy" are two words not typically used to describe knitwear. However, with the advent of knitstagram and the growing number of young people learning how to knit, that is quickly changing. Knitwear designers like myself have embraced this trend with open arms and have delved head first into creating warm weather patterns that are both comfortable for knitting *and* wearing.

In the heat of the summer, most knitters gravitate towards the most breathable options in their wardrobe. For myself, these are usually garments that either feature open stitchwork or are knit with plant-based fibers, both of which offer a cooling factor. It goes without saying that garments that expose more skin also fit the bill as well. This chapter features patterns that include all of the above and are also lightweight enough for knitting in the sun. Move over, beach reading. Beach knitting, it is!

The crochet-inspired Hollyberry Tee (page 113) and the Ivy Mesh coverup set (pages 91 and 97) patterns all feature lacework patterns that create airy fabrics to keep you cool on the hottest of days. Whether worn over a bralette or bathing suit, these designs provide endless layering options for both style and practical reasons. If open gauge coverups are not up your alley, both the Dahlia Bralette (page 85) and the Mariposa Top (page 107) are backless options perfect for lounging in the sun and beyond.

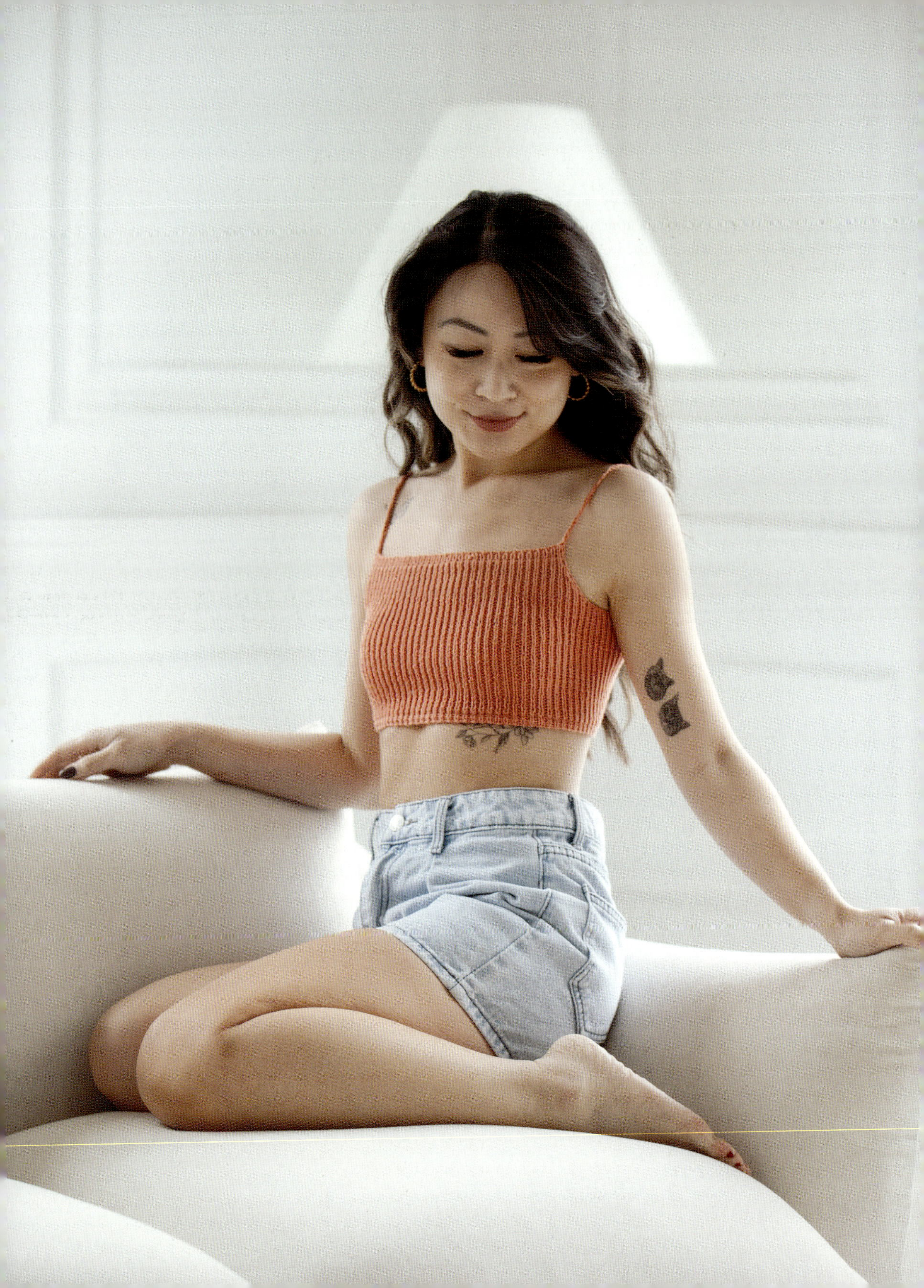

# Dahlia Bralette

The Dahlia Bralette is a teeny tiny top on trend with its open-back fastening. Knit in 1x1 ribbing throughout with a lightweight cotton yarn, the result is a stretchy fabric that will keep you cool in the hottest months of the year. Small enough to take with you on the go, the Dahlia Bralette is also the ideal project for mindless knitting while binge watching your favorite show. Perfect for a day out at the mall or an evening out with the girls, it can be dressed up or down. You can wear the bralette on its own with cargo pants and sneakers for a casual day out or layered under a blazer with linen trousers and kitten heels for a night on the town.

## Construction Notes

*The bralette is worked flat from the bottom up. Once the length of the body is established, stitches are bound off to create the sides. Further decreases are worked for the armholes until the front piece is completed. I-cord shoulder straps are worked and attached to the back piece and an additional set of I-cord back straps are picked up from each side of the top so it can be secured and tied together.*

## SKILL LEVEL
*Advanced Beginner*

## SIZING
XS (S, M, L, XL) (2XL, 3XL, 4XL, 5XL, 6XL)

15.75 (17.75, 20, 22, 23.75) (25.75, 28, 29.75, 31.75, 33.75)" / 40 (45, 51, 56, 61) (66, 71, 76, 81, 86) cm, blocked

## Materials

### Yarn
*DK weight, Paintbox Yarns Cotton DK in Vintage Pink (100% cotton), 137 yds (125 m) per 50-g skein*

*An alternate sample was also knit with Paintbox Yarns Cotton DK in Champagne White.*

*Any DK weight yarn can be used for this pattern as long as it matches gauge.*

## Yardage/Meterage
*145 (170, 195, 225, 250) (290, 340, 385, 445, 495) yds / 130 (155, 180, 205, 230) (265, 310, 350, 405, 450) m of DK weight yarn*

## Needles
**For ribbing:** *US 2 (2.75 mm) straight or circular needles*

**For body:** *US 4 (3.5 mm) straight or circular needles*

**For straps:** *US 4 (3.5 mm) straight, circular or double pointed needles*

## Notions
*Scissors*

*Tapestry needle*

## GAUGE
*35 sts x 31 rows = 4 inches (10 cm) in 1x1 ribbing worked flat using larger needles (blocked)*

## TECHNIQUES
*Double Stockinette Stitch (page 153)*

*I-Cord (page 153)*

# ABBREVIATIONS

| | |
|---|---|
| k | knit |
| p | purl |
| patt | pattern |
| rem | remain(ing) |
| rep | repeat |
| RS | right side |
| sl1wyif | slip 1 st purlwise with yarn in front |
| st(s) | stitch(es) |
| WS | wrong side |

# SCHEMATIC

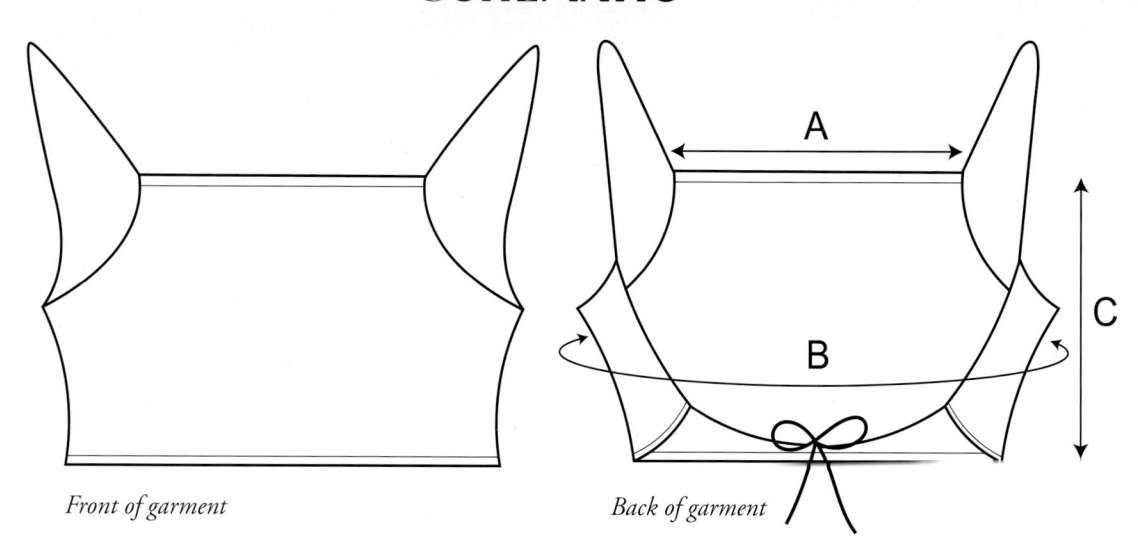

*Front of garment*

*Back of garment*

## SIZING CHART

|  | XS | S | M | L | XL | 2XL | 3XL | 4XL | 5XL | 6XL |  |
|---|---|---|---|---|---|---|---|---|---|---|---|
| A) Upper Top Width | 8 | 8.5 | 9 | 9.25 | 9.5 | 9.75 | 10.25 | 10.75 | 11 | 11.5 | in |
|  | 20 | 22 | 23 | 23 | 24 | 25 | 26 | 27 | 28 | 29 | cm |
| B) Lower Top Width | 15.75 | 17.75 | 20 | 22 | 23.75 | 25.75 | 28 | 29.75 | 31.75 | 33.75 | in |
|  | 40 | 45 | 51 | 56 | 61 | 66 | 71 | 76 | 81 | 86 | cm |
| C) Garment Length | 8.25 | 8.75 | 9 | 9.5 | 10 | 11 | 12.5 | 13.5 | 15 | 15.75 | in |
|  | 21 | 23 | 23 | 24 | 26 | 28 | 32 | 34 | 38 | 40 | cm |

The top is designed with -2 to 0 inches (-5 to 0 cm) of negative to neutral ease based on measurement B of the sizing chart. To select your ideal size, place a measuring tape beginning from one side of your body, over the largest part of your chest and then ending on the other side of your body. Sample shown is knit in size XS.

# DAHLIA BRALETTE PATTERN

## BODY

Using US 2 (2.75 mm) needles, cast on 138 (156, 174, 192, 208) (226, 244, 260, 278, 296) sts using the longtail cast on method.

**Row 1 (WS):** *K1, sl1wyif; rep from * until end.

**Rows 2–5:** Repeat row 1.

**Row 6 (RS):** K all sts.

Switch to US 4 (3.5 mm) needles.

**Row 7:** *K1, p1; rep from * until last 2 sts, k1, sl1wyif.

Festival & Beach Knits

**Row 2 (WS):** Bind off 28 (34, 40, 46, 52) (58, 62, 66, 70, 76) sts, work rem sts in patt until last 2 sts, p1, sl1wyif. [82 (88, 94, 100, 104) (110, 120, 128, 138, 144) sts rem]

**Row 3 (RS):** Slip 2 sts purlwise to the right needle. Slip first st over second st to bind off 1 st, work rem sts in patt until last 2 sts, p1, sl1wyif. [81 (87, 93, 99, 103) (109, 119, 127, 137, 143) sts rem]

**Row 4 (WS):** Slip 2 sts purlwise to the right needle. Slip first st over second st to bind off 1 st, work rem sts in patt until last 2 sts, p1, sl1wyif. [80 (86, 92, 98, 102) (108, 118, 126, 136, 142) sts rem]

**NOTE:** *In rows 3 & 4, you may be purling on a previous column of knit stitches before slipping the final stitch. In doing so, it creates a cleaner slipped edge.*

Repeat rows 3–4 a total of 4 (5, 6, 6, 8) (10, 13, 15, 19, 20) more times until 72 (76, 80, 86, 86) (88, 92, 96, 98, 102) sts rem.

**Next row:** Slip 2 sts purlwise to the right needle. Slip first st over second st to bind off 1 st, work rem sts in patt until last 2 sts, p1, sl1wyif. [71 (75, 79, 85, 85) (87, 91, 95, 97, 101) sts rem]

**Next row (WS):** Slip 2 sts purlwise to the right needle. Slip first st over second st to bind off 1 st, work rem sts in patt until last st, sl1wyif. [70 (74, 78, 84, 84) (86, 90, 94, 96, 100) sts rem]

Switch to US 2 (2.75 mm) needles.

**Next row (RS):** K until last st, sl1wyif.

**Next row (WS):** *K1, sl1wyif; rep from * until end.

Repeat last row 4 more times.

Repeat last row until piece measures 5.75 (6, 6, 6.5, 6.5) (7, 7.5, 8, 8.5, 9)" / 15 (15, 15, 17, 17) (18, 19, 20, 22, 23) cm from the cast on edge, or desired length for additional coverage. Your last row should be a WS row.

**NOTE:** *If a significant amount of length is added, it is recommended to add an additional set of back ties for security.*

## Begin Decreases

**Row 1 (RS):** Bind off 28 (34, 40, 46, 52) (58, 62, 66, 70, 76) sts, work rem sts in patt. [110 (122, 134, 146, 156) (168, 182, 194, 208, 220) sts rem]

**Next row (RS):** K2. Move those 2 sts you just worked to a holder or spare yarn to return to later. Bind off tightly in patt until there is only 1 st on the left needle. K the last st so that 2 sts rem. Slide sts to end of needle (or transfer them back to your left needle if you are using straight needles).

> **TIP:** *If you're having trouble binding off tightly, I recommend using just the tip of your needles to keep the sts taut.*

Switch to US 4 (3.5 mm) needles.

## RIGHT SHOULDER STRAP
**Next row:** K2. Slide sts to end of needle (or transfer back to left needle).

Repeat last row until strap measures 10 (10.25, 10.5, 10.5, 11) (11.5, 12.25, 12.75, 13.75, 14)" / 25 (26, 27, 27, 28) (29, 31, 32, 35, 36) cm or until desired length. Bind off and seam strap to the beginning of side bind offs.

## LEFT SHOULDER STRAP
Move 2 sts set aside earlier back to US 4 (3.5 mm) needle. Rejoin yarn to RS of work.

**Next row:** K2. Slide sts to end of needle (or transfer back to left needle).

Repeat last row until strap measures 10 (10.25, 10.5, 10.5, 11) (11.5, 12.25, 12.75, 13.75, 14)" / 25 (26, 27, 27, 28) (29, 31, 32, 35, 36) cm or until desired length to match right strap. Bind off and seam strap to the beginning of side bind offs.

## BACK LEFT STRAP
With the RS facing you and beginning from the bottommost st of the left body edge, rejoin yarn and use US 4 (3.5 mm) needles to pick up and k2. Slide sts to end of needle (or transfer back to left needle).

**Next row:** K2. Slide sts to end of needle (or transfer back to left needle).

Repeat last row until strap measures 12 (13, 14, 15, 16) (17, 18, 19.25, 20, 21)" / 30 (33, 36, 38, 41) (43, 46, 49, 51, 53) cm or until desired length. Bind off.

## BACK RIGHT STRAP
With the RS facing you and beginning from the st to the immediate right of the bottommost st of the right body edge, rejoin yarn and use US 4 (3.5 mm) needles to pick up and k2. Slide sts to end of needle (or transfer back to left needle).

Repeat last row until strap measures 12 (13, 14, 15, 16) (17, 18, 19.25, 20, 21)" / 30 (33, 36, 38, 41) (43, 46, 49, 51, 53) cm or until desired length. Bind off.

## FINISHING
Weave in any loose ends. Block your project using your preferred method.

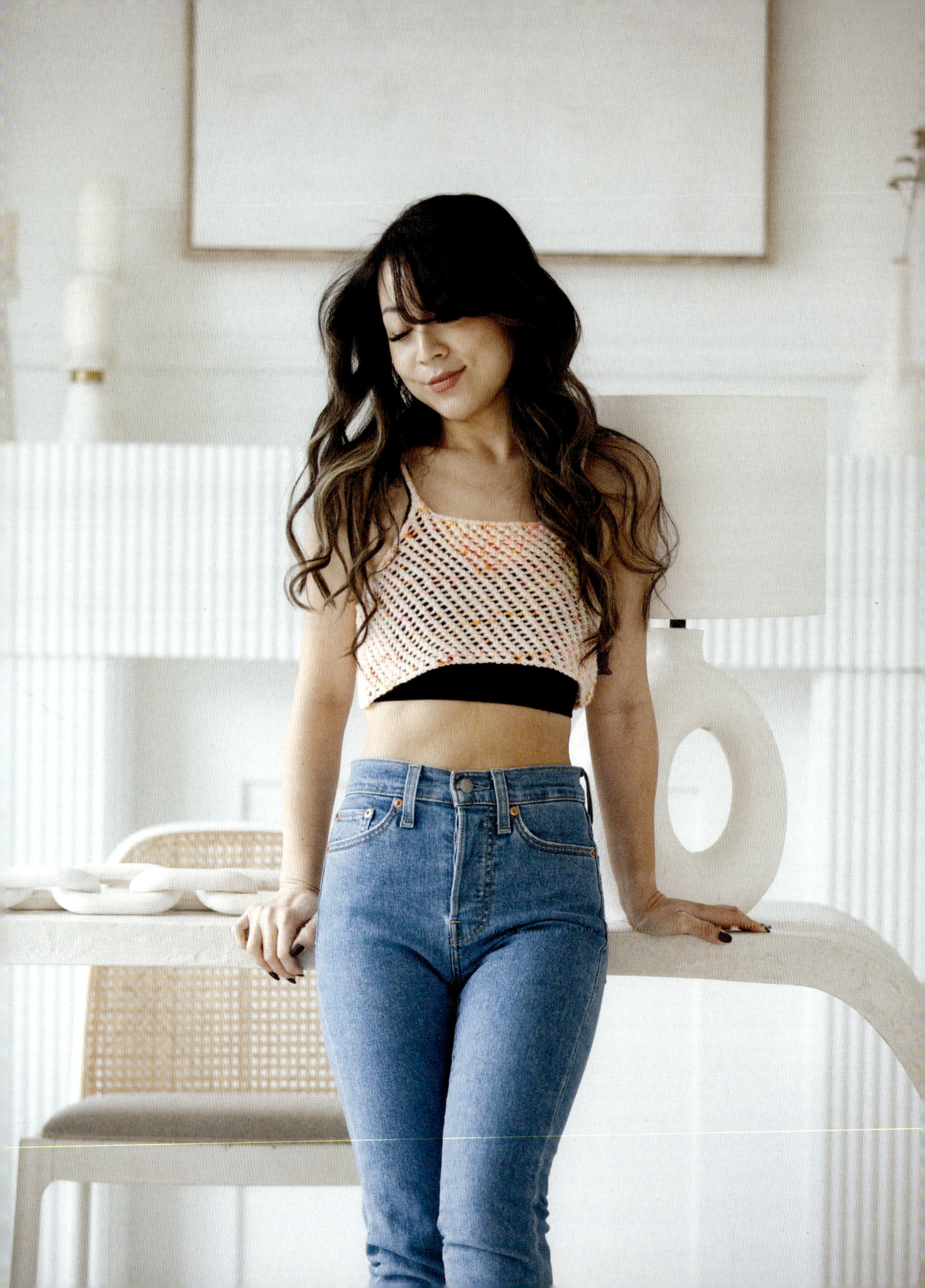

# Ivy Mesh Bralette

Whether you'll be lounging in a backyard pool or spending spring break at a resort, a swim coverup will inevitably be on your packing list. For my money, the perfect coverup is portable and lightweight with just enough coverage that your bathing suit can still be seen underneath. The outfit options are endless, but pairing it with the matching Ivy Mesh Skirt (page 97) would make the cutest beach ensemble. Alternatively, it can also be worn on a non-beach or pool day with a bralette underneath. Knit in a simple mesh lace stitch, the pattern suits both solid and variegated yarns. It also works up quickly, so you'll be showing this top off from sun up to sun down in no time.

## Construction Notes

The bralette is worked in the round from the bottom up before separating for front and back, and then each panel is worked flat. The front piece has additional rows that allow it to sit slightly higher than the back. I-cord straps are worked from stitches set aside from the front piece and are later seamed to the back.

## SKILL LEVEL
Advanced Beginner

## SIZING
XS (S, M, L, XL) (2XL, 3XL, 4XL, 5XL, 6XL)

Bust circumference of 28.75 (33, 36.25, 40.5, 44.75) (48, 52.25, 56.5, 60.75, 64)" / 73 (84, 92, 103, 114) (122, 133, 144, 155, 163) cm, blocked

## Materials

### Yarn
DK weight, Summer Camp Fibers Yarn Marshmallow DK in Fiesta (100% merino), 246 yds (225 m) per 100-g skein

Any DK weight yarn can be used for this pattern as long as it matches gauge.

### Yardage/Meterage
150 (200, 210, 275, 310) (345, 385, 445, 495, 535) yds / 135 (180, 190, 250, 280) (315, 350, 405, 450, 485) m of DK weight yarn

### Needles
**For body:** US 8 (5 mm), 24- to 60-inch (60- to 150-cm) circular needles

**For body cast on:** US 9 (5.5 mm), 24- to 60-inch (60- to 150-cm) circular needles

**For straps:** US 8 (5 mm) circular, straight or double pointed needles

### Notions
Stitch marker

Tapestry needle

### GAUGE
15 sts x 27.75 rounds = 4 inches (10 cm) in mesh lace st in the round using smaller needles (blocked)

### Mesh Lace Stitch (multiples of 2, worked in the round)
**Round 1:** K all sts
**Round 2:** *Sl1wyif, k1, psso, yo; rep from * until end.

### TECHNIQUES
Horizontal Invisible Seam (page 149)

I-Cord (page 153)

# ABBREVIATIONS

| | |
|---|---|
| BOR | beginning of round |
| DPN(s) | double pointed needle(s) |
| k | knit |
| k2tog | knit 2 sts together [1 st decreased] |
| p | purl |
| p2tog | purl 2 sts together [1 st decreased] |
| pm | place marker |
| psso | pass slipped stitch over |
| rem | remain(ing) |
| rep | repeat |
| RS | right side |
| sl1wyib | slip 1 st purlwise with yarn in back |
| sl1wyif | slip 1 st purlwise with yarn in front |
| ssk | slip 2 sts knitwise, one at a time; move both stitches back to the left needle; knit these 2 sts together through the back loops [1 st decreased] |
| st(s) | stitch(es) |
| stm(s) | stitch marker(s) |
| WS | wrong side |
| yo | yarnover |

## SIZING CHART

|  | XS | S | M | L | XL | 2XL | 3XL | 4XL | 5XL | 6XL |  |
|---|---|---|---|---|---|---|---|---|---|---|---|
| A) Body Circumference | 28.75 | 33 | 36.25 | 40.5 | 44.75 | 48 | 52.25 | 56.5 | 60.75 | 64 | in |
|  | 73 | 84 | 92 | 103 | 114 | 122 | 133 | 144 | 155 | 163 | cm |
| B) Body Length | 9 | 9.75 | 10.25 | 11.25 | 12 | 12.75 | 12.75 | 14.25 | 14.25 | 14.75 | in |
|  | 23 | 25 | 26 | 29 | 30 | 32 | 32 | 37 | 37 | 38 | cm |
| C) Underarm Height | 3.5 | 3.75 | 4.25 | 4.75 | 5.5 | 5.75 | 5.75 | 6.75 | 6.75 | 6.75 | in |
|  | 9 | 10 | 11 | 12 | 14 | 15 | 15 | 18 | 18 | 18 | cm |

*The top is designed with -2 to 1 inches (-5 to 3 cm) of negative to positive ease. Sample shown is knit in size XS. If in between sizes, select the smaller size, as there is a lot of stretch in this project (can stretch up to 20% larger).*

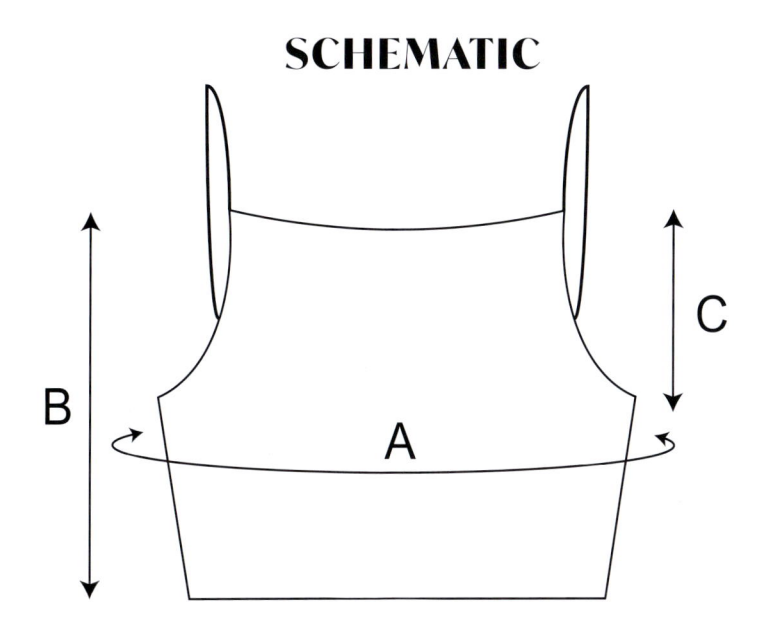

## SCHEMATIC

## IVY MESH BRALETTE PATTERN

### BODY

Using US 9 (5.5 mm) needles, cast on 108 (124, 136, 152, 168) (180, 196, 212, 228, 240) sts using the longtail cast on method. Pm and join for working in the round.

Switch to US 8 (5 mm) needles.

**Round 1:** K all sts.

**Round 2:** Sl1wyib, k1, psso, yo, *sl1wyif, k1, psso, yo; rep from * until end.

Repeat rounds 1–2 a total of 17 (19, 19, 21, 21) (23, 23, 24, 24, 26) more times.

**NOTE:** Since this stitch will grow significantly after blocking, I suggest counting rows rather than measuring for length. For roughly every 1 inch (3 cm) of length you wish added to the body length, repeat the 2-round stitch 3 more times.

**Next round:** K54 (62, 68, 76, 84) (90, 98, 106, 114, 120), pm for side, k54 (62, 68, 76, 84) (90, 98, 106, 114, 120).

### Separate for Front/Back

**NOTE:** When binding off the sts for the underarm, the final bound off st on your right hand needle will be considered the first st in the following instructions.

**Row 1 (RS):** Remove BOR stm. Bind off 4 (4, 6, 6, 6) (8, 8, 10, 10, 12) sts, k2, *yo, sl1wyif, k1, psso; rep from * until 4 (4, 6, 6, 6) (8, 8, 10, 10, 12) sts before side stm, k4 (4, 6, 6, 6) (8, 8, 10, 10, 12). Remove side stm and leave rem 54 (62, 68, 76, 84) (90, 98, 106, 114, 120) sts on a holder or spare yarn to return to later. [50 (58, 62, 70, 78) (82, 90, 96, 104, 108) sts rem]

**Row 2 (WS):** Bind off 4 (4, 6, 6, 6) (8, 8, 10, 10, 12) sts, p until end. [46 (54, 56, 64, 72) (74, 82, 86, 94, 96) sts rem]

**Row 3:** Sl1wyib, ssk, *yo, sl1wyif, k1, psso; rep from * until last 3 sts, k2tog, k1. [44 (52, 54, 62, 70) (72, 80, 84, 92, 94) sts rem, 2 sts decreased]

**Row 4:** Sl1wyif, p until end.

Repeat rows 3–4 a total of 5 (6, 6, 8, 8) (9, 9, 11, 11, 11) more times until 34 (40, 42, 46, 54) (54, 62, 62, 70, 72) sts rem.

**Next row (RS):** Sl1wyib, k2, *yo, sl1wyif, k1, psso; rep from * until last st, k1.

**Next row (WS):** Sl1wyif, p until end.

**Next row:** Sl1wyib, k1, *yo, sl1wyif, k1, psso; rep from * until last 2 sts, k2.

**Next row:** Sl1wyif, p until end.

Repeat last 4 rows a total of 1 (1, 2, 2, 3) (3, 3, 4, 4, 4) more time(s).

### Create Neck Opening

**Next row (RS):** Sl1wyib, k2, yo, sl1wyif, k1, psso, k1, bind off 22 (28, 30, 34, 42) (42, 50, 50, 58, 60) sts very loosely, k2, yo, sl1wyif, k1, psso, k1. You should have 6 sts on each side of the neckline. Move the 6 live sts for the front left strap to a holder or spare yarn to return to later.

## FRONT RIGHT

**Next row (WS):** Sl1wyif, p5.

**Next row (RS):** Sl1wyib, ssk, k3. [5 sts rem]

**Next row:** Sl1wyif, p4.

**Next row:** Sl1wyib, ssk, k2. [4 sts rem]

**Next row:** Sl1wyif, p3.

**Next row:** Sl1wyib, ssk, k1. [3 sts rem]

At this point, feel free to switch to DPNs or shorter circular needles. Slide sts to end of needle (or transfer back to left needle).

**Next row:** K3. Slide sts to end of needle (or transfer back to left needle).

Repeat last row until strap measures 12 inches (30 cm) or until desired length. Bind off and break yarn, leaving an 8-inch (20-cm) tail for joining later. Set aside to return to later.

## FRONT LEFT

Rejoin yarn to WS of work. Pick up the far right st and place it on your left-hand needle [7 sts]. By picking up a st from the front bind off, it will result in a cleaner finish between the two sides of the front.

**Next row (WS):** P2tog, p5. [6 sts rem]

**Next row (RS):** Sl1wyib, k2, k2tog, k1. [5 sts rem]

**Next row:** Sl1wyif, p4.

**Next row:** Sl1wyib, k1, k2tog, k1. [4 sts rem]

**Next row:** Sl1wyif, p3.

**Next row:** Sl1wyib, k2tog, k1. [3 sts rem]

Festival & Beach Knits

Slide sts to end of needle (or transfer back to left needle).

**Next row:** K3. Slide sts to end of needle (or transfer back to left needle).

Repeat last row until strap measures 12 inches (30 cm) or matches the length of the front right strap. Bind off and break yarn, leaving an 8-inch (20-cm) tail for joining later. Set aside to return to later.

## BACK

Rejoin yarn to RS of work. Pick up the leftmost st from the front bind offs and slip it over the first st from the backside to create a seamless transition from the front and back pieces.

**Row 1 (RS):** Bind off 4 (4, 6, 6, 6) (8, 8, 10, 10, 12) sts, k2, *yo, sl1wyif, k1, psso; rep from * until last 4 (4, 6, 6, 6) (8, 8, 10, 10, 12) sts, k4 (4, 6, 6, 6) (8, 8, 10, 10, 12). [50 (58, 62, 70, 78) (82, 90, 96, 104, 108) sts rem]

> **NOTE:** *Like the front underarm bindoffs, the final bound off st on your right-hand needle will be considered the first st in the following instructions.*

**Row 2 (WS):** Pick up the leftmost st from the front bind offs and slip it over the first st of the next row. Bind off 4 (4, 6, 6, 6) (8, 8, 10, 10, 12) sts, p until end. [46 (54, 56, 64, 72) (74, 82, 86, 94, 96) sts rem]

**Row 3:** Sl1wyib, ssk, *yo, sl1wyif, k1, psso; rep from * until last 3 sts, k2tog, k1. [44 (52, 54, 62, 70) (72, 80, 84, 92, 94) sts rem, 2 sts decreased]

**Row 4:** Sl1wyif, p until end.

Repeat rows 3–4 a total of 5 (6, 6, 8, 8) (9, 9, 11, 11, 11) more times until 34 (40, 42, 46, 54) (54, 62, 62, 70, 72) sts rem.

**Next row (RS):** Bind off all sts loosely.

### Joining Straps

With the RS facing, use horizontal invisible seaming technique to join the straps to the back.

## FINISHING

Weave in any loose ends. Block your project using your preferred method.

# Ivy Mesh Skirt

Along with a bikini top, a matching skirt is a summer essential. The full-length Ivy Mesh Skirt is lightweight enough to easily pack in any getaway bag. Although versatile enough to wear with a variety of coverup tops, the perfect accompaniment is the Ivy Mesh Bralette (page 91). Knit in the same lace pattern, the resulting garment is durable and pleasant to wear even on the hottest of summer days.

The open nature of the pattern ensures the skirt will feel airy and comfortable regardless of your choice of fiber content. The repetitive nature of the pattern also makes it relatively speedy to knit despite the size of the project. The drawstring allows you to adjust for your perfect fit at the waist and the tassels add a touch of playfulness to the outfit.

## Construction Notes

*The skirt is worked from the top down, beginning with a folded hem. The skirt is knit in the round in a mesh lace stitch until a side slit is created, after which the remainder of the skirt is worked flat. An I-cord is worked to create the drawstring for the skirt, and lastly two tassels are made using the same yarn and attached to both ends.*

## SKILL LEVEL
*Advanced Beginner*

## SIZING
XS (S, M, L, XL) (2XL, 3XL, 4XL, 5XL, 6XL)

Waist circumference of 24.5 (26.75, 29, 32, 35.75) (39.5, 43.5, 48, 49.5, 52.5)" / 62 (68, 74, 81, 91) (101, 110, 122, 126, 134) cm, blocked

## Materials

### Yarn
DK weight, Summer Camp Fibers Yarn Marshmallow DK in Fiesta (100% merino), 246 yds (225 m) per 100-g skein

Any DK weight yarn can be used for this pattern as long as it matches gauge.

## Yardage/Meterage
685 (750, 810, 930, 1040) (1150, 1305, 1440, 1535, 1625) yds / 625 (685, 740, 850, 950) (1050, 1190, 1315, 1400, 1485) m of DK weight yarn

## Needles

**For waistband:** US 6 (4 mm), 24- to 60-inch (60- to 150-cm) circular needles

**For skirt:** US 9 (5.5 mm), 24- to 60-inch (60- to 150-cm) circular needles

**For drawstring:** US 4 (3.5 mm) straight or double pointed needles

## Notions
Cardboard for making tassels (optional)

Crochet hook (US 6–8 / 4–5 mm)

Piece of cardboard or cardstock

Ruler

Safety pin

Scissors

Sewing needle and matching thread

Stitch marker

Tapestry needle

## GAUGE
21 sts x 24 rounds = 4 inches (10 cm) in stockinette st in the round using US 6 (4 mm) needles (blocked)

14 sts x 24 rounds = 4 inches (10 cm) in mesh lace st in the round using largest needles (blocked)

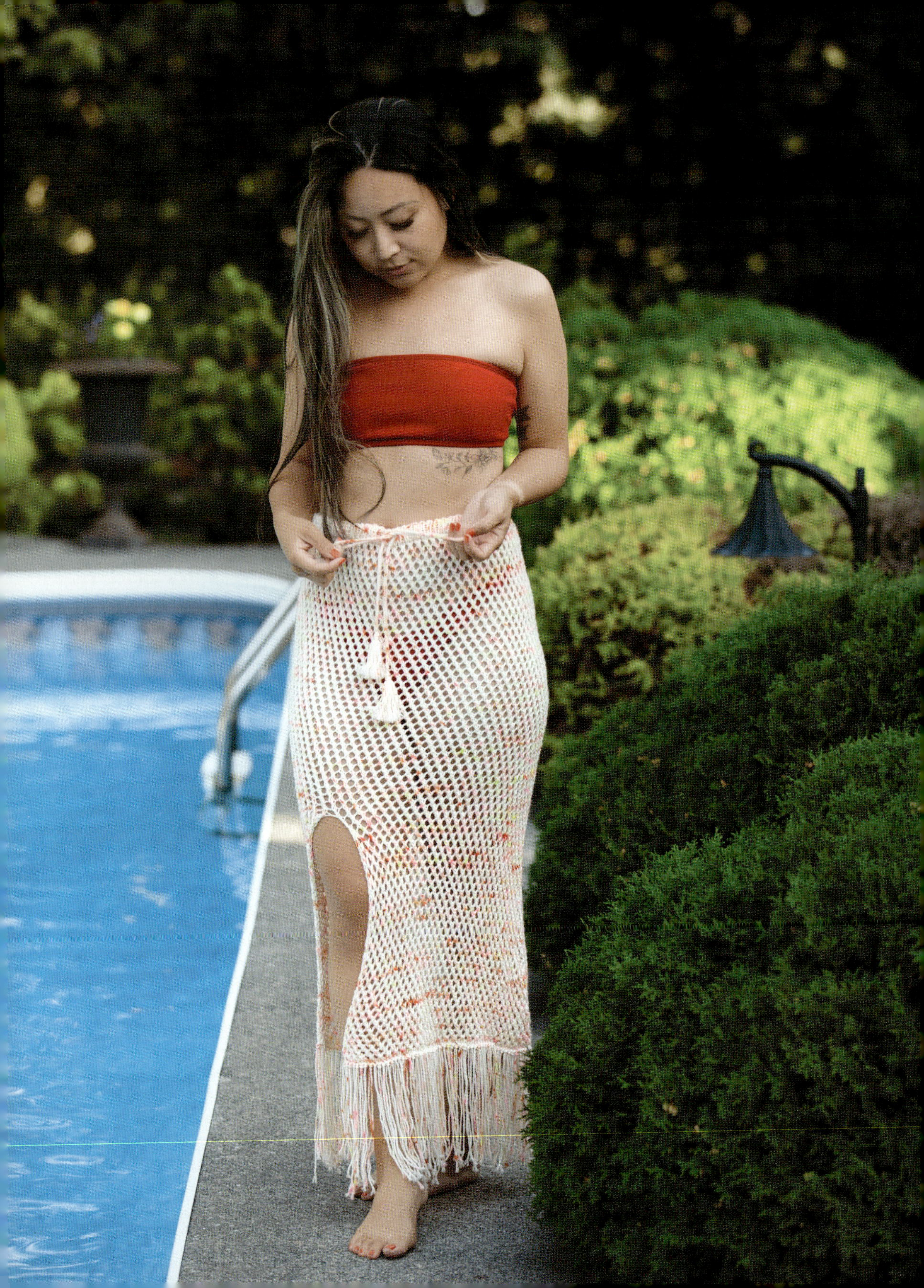

**Mesh Lace Stitch (multiples of 2, worked in the round)**

**Round 1:** *K all sts*

**Round 2:** *Sl1wyif, k1, psso, yo; rep from * until end.*

**TECHNIQUES**

*I-Cord (page 153)*

*Tassels (instructions within pattern)*

*Fringe (page 152)*

## ABBREVIATIONS

| | |
|---|---|
| BOR | beginning of round |
| CSD | centered single decrease: slip 2 sts knitwise (one after another); insert the left needle into the front of both slipped stitches, knit together; insert the left needle into the second of the just decreased stitches, placing it onto the left needle, ready to be worked; insert the right needle into the next 2 sts to k2tog [1 st decreased] |
| double yo | yarnover twice |
| k | knit |
| k2tog | knit 2 sts together [1 st decreased] |
| p | purl |
| p1tbl | purl through the back loop |
| patt | pattern |
| pm | place marker |
| psso | pass slipped stitch over |
| rep | repeat |
| RS | right side |
| sl1wyib | slip 1 st purlwise with yarn in back |
| sl1wyif | slip 1 st purlwise with yarn in front |
| st(s) | stitch(es) |
| stm(s) | stitch marker(s) |
| WS | wrong side |
| yo | yarnover |

## SIZING CHART

|  | XS | S | M | L | XL | 2XL | 3XL | 4XL | 5XL | 6XL |  |
|---|---|---|---|---|---|---|---|---|---|---|---|
| A) Waist Circumference | 24.5 | 26.75 | 29 | 32 | 35.75 | 39.5 | 43.5 | 48 | 49.5 | 52.5 | in |
|  | 62 | 68 | 74 | 81 | 91 | 101 | 110 | 122 | 126 | 134 | cm |
| B) Hip Circumference | 36.5 | 40 | 43.5 | 48 | 53.75 | 59.5 | 65.25 | 72 | 74.25 | 78.75 | in |
|  | 93 | 102 | 110 | 122 | 137 | 151 | 166 | 183 | 189 | 200 | cm |
| C) Garment Length | 27.25 | 27.25 | 27.25 | 28.25 | 28.25 | 28.25 | 29.5 | 29.5 | 30.5 | 30.5 | in |
|  | 69 | 69 | 69 | 72 | 72 | 72 | 75 | 75 | 77 | 77 | cm |

The skirt is designed with -2 to 2 inches (-5 to 5 cm) of negative to positive ease at the waist. Sample shown is knit in size S. If in between sizes, select the smaller size, as there is a lot of stretch in this project (can stretch up to 20% larger).

## SCHEMATIC

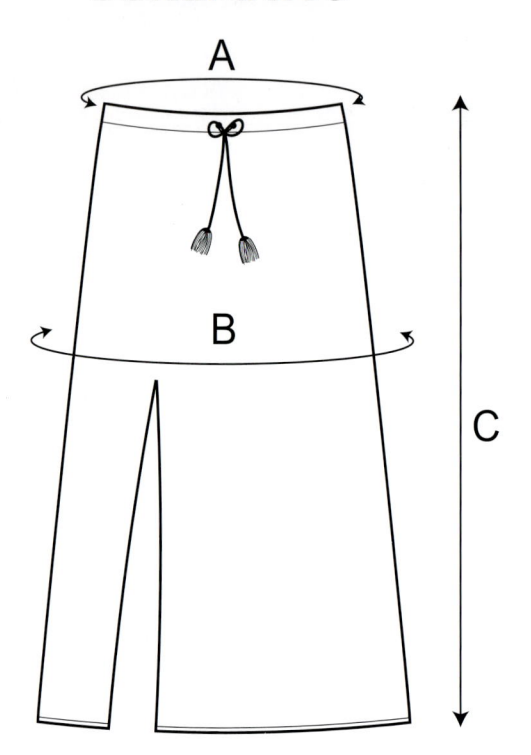

Light & Breezy Knitwear

# IVY MESH SKIRT PATTERN

## TOP HEM
Using US 6 (4 mm) needles, cast on 128 (140, 152, 168, 188) (208, 228, 252, 260, 276) sts using the longtail cast on method. Pm and join for working in the round.

**Rounds 1–5:** *K1, p1; rep from * until end.

**Round 6 (turning round):** P all sts.

**Rounds 7–9:** *K1, p1; rep from * until end.

**Round 10:** Work 27 (30, 33, 37, 42) (47, 52, 58, 60, 64) sts in 1x1 rib, double yo, CSD, work 4 sts in patt, CSD, double yo, work remainder of round in 1x1 rib patt.

**Round 11:** *K1, p1; rep from * until end, maintaining the patt even over the yos and decreases from the round below. Work those sts tightly to ensure no gaps.

**Round 12:** *K1, p1; rep from * until end.

### Join to Create a Folded Hem
Fold your work so that the purl round is at the bottom and the cast on edge is behind your current round (the drawstring openings should be on the RS facing out). You are now going to knit the next round with the cast on edge. Pick up the first stitch of the cast on edge and move it to your left-hand needle. Knit this stitch together with the first stitch in your current round.

Repeat this step until all the stitches on the cast on edge have been picked up and knit together with your current round. Your hem is now complete.

## BODY
Switch to US 9 (5.5 mm) needles.

**Round 1:** K all sts.

**Round 2:** Sl1wyib, k1, psso, yo, *sl1wyif, k1, psso, yo; rep from * until end.

> **NOTE:** *Since this stitch grows significantly after blocking, I suggest counting rows rather than measuring for length at this point. If your gauge is accurate, the length of your skirt will match the sizing chart.*
>
> *For every 1 inch (3 cm) of length you wish added to the skirt length, repeat the 2-round stitch 3 more times. Alternatively, you may also shorten the skirt to better suit your preferred length.*

Repeat rounds 1–2 a total of 41 (41, 41, 42, 42) (42, 43, 43, 44, 44) more times for a total of 84 (84, 84, 86, 86) (86, 88, 88, 90, 90) rounds worked.

If you do not wish to create a side slit, continue repeating rounds 1–2 until you reach your desired length. However, note that your mobility may be limited! For roughly every 1 inch (3 cm) of added length, repeat the 2-round stitch 3 more times.

## Create Side Slit

Remove BOR stm and turn work so the WS is facing you. You will now be working flat.

> **NOTE:** Since the mesh stitch slants left, be mindful that the side slit won't remain on the side of your body as the rounds progress.

**Row 1 (WS):** P1tbl, p until end.

**Row 2 (RS):** Sl1wyib, k1, *yo, sl1wyif, k1, psso, rep from * until last 2 sts, k2.

**Row 3:** Sl1wyif, p until end.

**Row 4:** Sl1wyib, k2, *yo, sl1wyif, k1, psso, rep from * until last st, k1.

**Row 5:** Sl1wyif, p until end.

Repeat rows 2–5 a total of 17 (17, 17, 18, 18) (18, 19, 19, 20, 20) more times for a total of 73 (73, 73, 77, 77) (77, 81, 81, 85, 85) rounds worked.

Bind off all sts loosely.

## I-CORD DRAWSTRING

Leaving a 5-inch (13-cm) tail and using US 4 (3.5 mm) needles, cast on 2 sts using the long-tail cast on method. Slide sts to end of needle (or transfer back to left needle).

**Next row:** K2. Slide sts to end of needle (or transfer back to left needle).

Repeat last row until drawstring measures 35 (37, 40, 44, 48) (52, 56, 58, 61, 63)" / 89 (94, 102, 112, 122) (133, 143, 148, 155, 161) cm or until desired length. Bind off, leaving a 5-inch (13-cm) tail to tie the tassel after. Secure a safety pin to one end of your cord and feed it into one of the openings of your waistband until it comes out the other opening.

## TASSELS (MAKE 2)

For this step, you will need a piece of cardboard, a ruler and a pair of scissors (Image 1). Measure and cut a piece of cardboard that measures approximately 2 inches (5 cm) wide and double the height of the desired length of your tassel.

Wrap your yarn lengthwise around the cardboard a total of 6 times (Image 2). Cut your yarn and gently slide the bundle of yarn off of the cardboard (Image 3).

Measure and mark the center of the bundle (Image 4). Taking the tail of one end of your drawstring, tie a double knot in the center of the bundle (Image 5). Ensure there is no gap between the end of the I-cord and the yarn bundle. Once the bundle is secured, cut both ends of the bundle so there are individual strands of yarn (Image 6). Position the tassel so the loose ends are at the bottom of the I-cord.

Cut a piece of yarn approximately 10 inches (25 cm) long. Fold it in half and position it parallel to the tassel, with the folded end facing the tassel ends, approximately 1 inch (3 cm) below the I-cord (Image 7, page 104).

Image 1

Image 2

Image 3

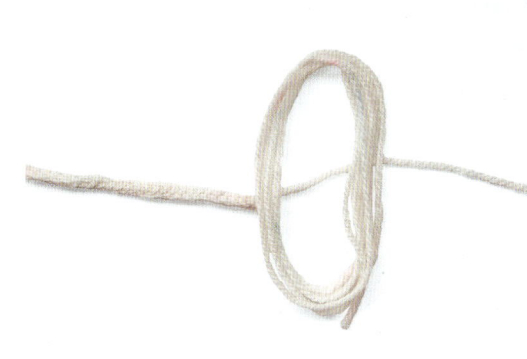

Image 4

Image 5

Image 6

**Festival & Beach Knits**

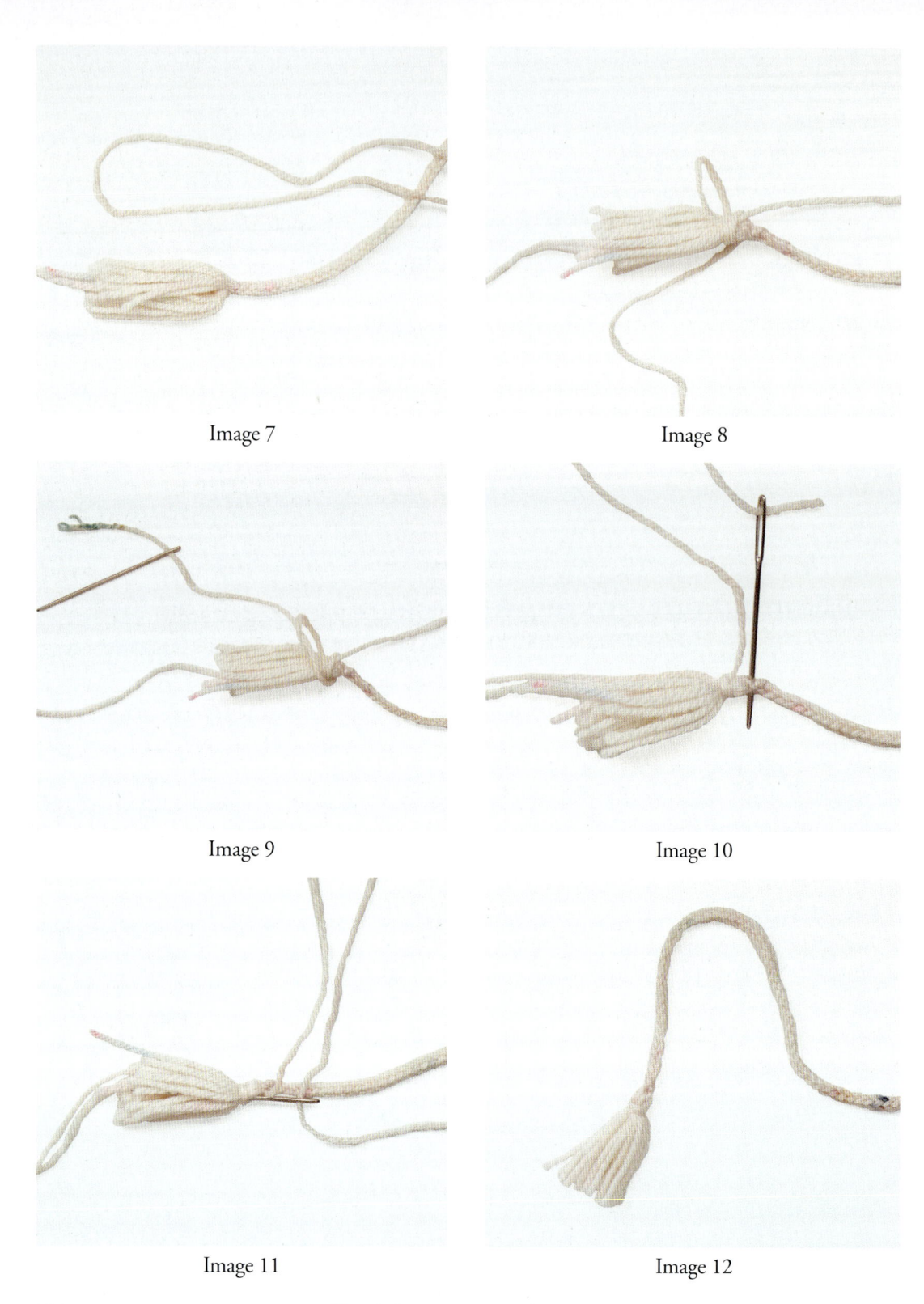

Image 7

Image 8

Image 9

Image 10

Image 11

Image 12

104  Light & Breezy Knitwear

Holding the loop and the tassel ends securely using one hand, use your other hand to tightly wrap one end of the tail around the yarn bundle (approximately 0.25 inch [1 cm] below the drawstring) a total of 4 times (Image 8). After the fourth wrap, use a tapestry needle as a guide and insert the tail into the loop at the top of the bundle and pull it towards the bottom of the tassel (Image 9). Pull the other tail so that the wrap around the tassel is secure. One end of the tail is now hidden among the tassel ends.

We will now secure and hide the other end of the tail used to wrap the tassel. Using a tapestry needle, insert the remaining end up towards the point where the tassel meets the I-cord and then back down and under the wraps (Images 10 & 11).

Use a pair of sharp scissors to trim the tassel ends so they are nice and even (Image 12).

## FRINGE
Cut 128 (140, 152, 168, 188) (208, 228, 252, 260, 276) strands of yarn that measure 10 inches (26 cm) each.

You will now be attaching one fringe to each bound off stitch along the entire bottom edge.

With the RS of the skirt facing you, insert a crochet hook into a bind off edge st from the inside out. Fold the strand of yarn and place the middle onto the hook. Use the hook to pull the strand of yarn about 1 inch (3 cm) inside the garment. Use your other hand to insert the tail ends of the yarn into the loop you've created. Use the crochet hook (or your hands) to pull the remainder of the tail inside, and tighten. Repeat this step for the remaining bind off sts.

If you wish, trim the ends using a pair of sharp scissors to ensure the fringe is even.

## FINISHING
Weave in any loose ends. Block your project. I recommend wet blocking the skirt so the stitches bloom and grow to the correct gauge. The tassel and fringe also look more polished after a light spray as well!

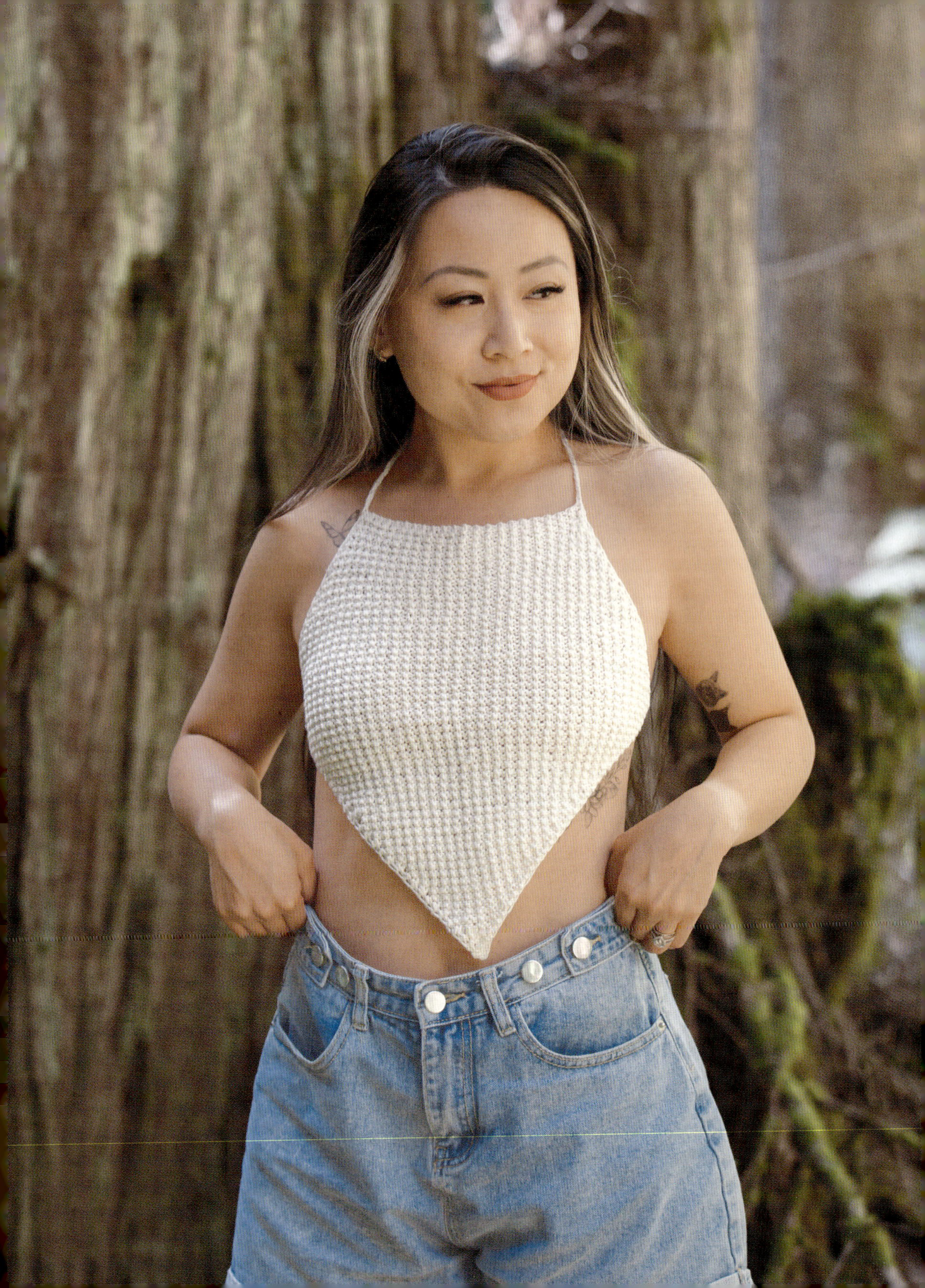

# Mariposa Top

As much as some may want it to disappear, Y2K fashion is here to stay and I am all for it. Rather than going out and buying a bandana to re-create this look, look no further because this pattern will re-create the vibe without risking a possible wardrobe malfunction. Gone are the days of tying a bandana around your chest as tightly as you can while crossing your fingers that everything is secure.

Simple in construction and requiring just a scant amount of yarn, the Mariposa Top will knit up so quickly you will definitely be tempted to make more than one. The pattern is knit entirely in rice stitch, creating a bumpy fabric that is both eye-catching and engaging to knit. The design lends itself really well to all types of yarns, whether variegated or even textured. The sample is photographed with the "bumpy" side out, but the versatile rice stitch looks equally beautiful from the wrong side. Just make sure your ends are woven in nicely and you can wear it whichever way you want.

## Construction Notes

The top is worked flat from the top down, beginning with the neckline. You will increase stitches until you achieve full frontal coverage. Once all the increases are completed, you will begin decreases immediately to create a tapered triangular shape. Note, the decreases are worked more aggressively compared to the increases in order to create a sharp point. Lastly, stitches are picked up from both sides of the neckline as well as the sides to create the neck and side straps.

## SKILL LEVEL
Beginner

## SIZING
XS (S, M, L, XL) (2XL, 3XL, 4XL, 5XL, 6XL)

Circumference at the widest part of bust 16.25 (18.5, 21, 23.25, 25.5) (27.75, 30.25, 32.5, 34.75, 37)" / 41 (47, 53, 59, 65) (71, 77, 83, 88, 94) cm, blocked

## Materials

### Yarn
Worsted weight, Drops Design Bomull-Lin in Off White (53% cotton, 47% cellulose [linen/flax]), 93 yds (85 m) per 50-g skein

Any DK or worsted weight yarn can be used for this pattern as long as it matches gauge.

## Yardage/Meterage
145 (170, 225, 295, 320) (345, 450, 535, 625, 690) yds / 130 (155, 205, 270, 290) (315, 410, 485, 570, 630) m of DK or worsted weight yarn

## Needles
**For body:** US 6 (4 mm) straight or circular needles

**For straps:** US 4 (3.5 mm) straight or double pointed needles

## Notions
Removable stitch markers

Tapestry needle

## GAUGE
22 sts x 32 rows = 4 inches (10 cm) in rice stitch worked flat using larger needles (blocked)

## Rice Stitch (multiples of 2+1)
**Row 1 (RS):** P1, *k1tbl, p1; rep from * until end.

**Row 2 (WS):** K all sts.

## TECHNIQUES
I-Cord (page 153)

**FESTIVAL & BEACH KNITS**

# ABBREVIATIONS

| | |
|---|---|
| CDD | centered double decrease: slip 2 sts together knitwise; knit 1 st; using the tip of your left needle, pick up the 2 sts you slipped and pass them over the knitted st and off of the needle [2 sts decreased] |
| dec | decrease |
| k | knit |
| k1tbl | knit through the back loop |
| k2sp | knit 2 sts together; slip the knitted st back to the left needle purlwise; insert the right needle into the front leg of the second st on the left needle and pass it over the first stitch and off the left needle; slip the completed stitch purlwise back to the right needle [2 sts decreased] |
| k2tog | knit 2 sts together [1 st decreased] |
| kfb | knit 1 st but do not remove it from the left needle; knit 1 st into the back loop of the same st, remove the st from the left needle [1 st increased] |
| inc | increase |
| p | purl |
| p1tbl | purl through the back loop |
| rem | remain(ing) |
| rep | repeat |
| RS | right side |
| sl1kw | slip 1 st knitwise |
| sl1wyif | slip 1 st purlwise with yarn in front |
| ssk | slip 2 sts knitwise, one at a time; move both stitches back to the left needle; knit these 2 sts together through the back loops [1 st decreased] |
| st(s) | stitch(es) |
| stm(s) | stitch marker(s) |
| sk2p | slip 1 st knitwise from left to right needle; knit 2 sts together; insert the left needle into the front leg of the second st on the right needle and pass it over the first stitch and off the right needle [2 sts decreased] |
| WS | wrong side |
| wyib | with yarn in back |

Light & Breezy Knitwear

## SIZING CHART

|  | XS | S | M | L | XL | 2XL | 3XL | 4XL | 5XL | 6XL |  |
|---|---|---|---|---|---|---|---|---|---|---|---|
| A) Upper Top Width | 8.25 | 9.25 | 10.25 | 11.5 | 12.5 | 13.75 | 15 | 16.25 | 17.25 | 18.25 | in |
|  | 21 | 24 | 26 | 29 | 32 | 35 | 38 | 41 | 44 | 46 | cm |
| B) Widest Part of Top | 16.25 | 18.5 | 21 | 23.25 | 25.5 | 27.75 | 30.25 | 32.5 | 34.75 | 37 | in |
|  | 41 | 47 | 53 | 59 | 65 | 71 | 77 | 83 | 89 | 94 | cm |
| C) Garment Length | 18.25 | 20.75 | 24 | 26.75 | 29.25 | 29.25 | 34.75 | 37.5 | 40.75 | 43.25 | in |
|  | 46 | 53 | 61 | 68 | 74 | 74 | 88 | 95 | 103 | 110 | cm |

To select your size, measure the widest part of your bust from one side to the other. The top is designed with 0 to 1 inch (0 to 3 cm) of neutral to positive ease. Sample shown is knit in size XS. If in between sizes, it is recommended to select the smaller size.

## SCHEMATIC

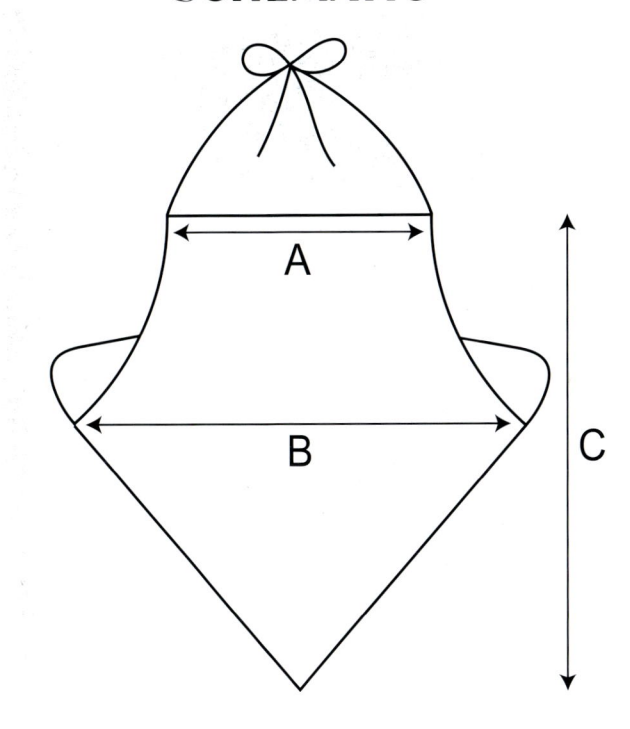

# MARIPOSA TOP PATTERN

## TOP

Using US 6 (4 mm) needles, cast on 45 (51, 57, 63, 69) (75, 83, 89, 95, 101) sts using the longtail cast on method.

**Row 1 (RS):** Sl1wyif, *k1tbl, p1; rep from * until last 2 sts, k1tbl, p1tbl.

**Row 2 (WS, inc):** Sl1kw wyib, kfb, k until last 2 sts, kfb, k1tbl. [47 (53, 59, 65, 71) (77, 85, 91, 97, 103) sts, 2 sts increased]

**Row 3:** Sl1wyif, p1, *k1tbl, p1; rep from * until last st, k1.

**Row 4 (inc):** Sl1wyif, kfb, k until last 2 sts, kfb, k1. [49 (55, 61, 67, 73) (79, 87, 93, 99, 105) sts, 2 sts increased]

Repeat rows 1–4 a total of 10 (11, 13, 15, 16) (16, 19, 21, 23, 24) more times until you have a total of 89 (99, 113, 127, 137) (143, 163, 177, 191, 201) sts. Place a removable stm at both ends of the row.

## Begin Decreases

**Row 1 (RS, dec):** Sl1wyif, sk2p, *p1, k1tbl; rep from * until last 4 sts, k2sp, p1tbl. [85 (95, 109, 123, 133) (139, 159, 173, 187, 197) sts, 4 sts decreased]

**Row 2 (WS):** Sl1kw wyib, k until end.

**Row 3:** Sl1wyif, ssk, *k1tbl, p1, rep from * until last 3 sts, k2tog, p1tbl. [83 (93, 107, 121, 131) (137, 157, 171, 185, 195) sts, 2 sts decreased]

**Row 4:** Sl1kw wyib, k until end.

**Row 5:** Sl1wyif, ssk, p1, *k1tbl, p1; rep from * until last 3 sts, k2tog, k1. [81 (91, 105, 119, 129) (135, 155, 169, 183, 193) sts, 2 sts decreased]

**Row 6:** Sl1wyif, k until end.

Repeat rows 1–6 a total of 9 (11, 12, 14, 15) (16, 19, 20, 22, 23) more times until 9 (3, 9, 7, 9) (7, 3, 9, 7, 9) sts rem.

*Sizes XS, M, XL, 4XL & 6XL only*
**Next row (RS, dec):** Sl1wyif, ssk, *k1tbl, p1, k1tbl, k2tog, p1tbl. [7 sts, 2 sts decreased]

**Next row (WS):** Sl1kw wyib, k6.

**Next row:** Sl1wyif, ssk, p1, k2tog, k1. [5 sts, 2 sts decreased]

**Next row:** Sl1wyif, k4.

**Next row:** Sl1wyif, CDD, k1.

**Next row:** Sl1wyif, k2. [3 sts, 2 sts decreased]

*Sizes L, 2XL & 5XL only*
**Next row (RS, dec):** Sl1wyif, ssk, p1, k2tog, k1. [5 sts, 2 sts decreased]

**Next row (WS):** Sl1wyif, k4.

**Next row:** Sl1wyif, CDD, k1.

**Next row:** Sl1wyif, k2. [3 sts, 2 sts decreased]

*All sizes resume*
Bind off all sts.

## TOP STRAPS

> **TIP:** *The following instructions are suggested placements for the top straps. Feel free to use a long piece of yarn to test out placement prior to continuing.*

### Top Right Neck Strap

With the RS facing you and using US 4 (3.5 mm) needles, identify the second cast on st from the left and pick up and k2.

**Next row:** K2. Slide sts to end of needle (or transfer back to left needle).

Repeat last row until strap measures 24 inches (61 cm) or until desired length. Bind off.

### Top Left Neck Strap

With the RS facing you and using US 4 (3.5 mm) needles, identify the last cast on st from the right and pick up and k2.

**Next row:** K2. Slide sts to end of needle (or transfer back to left needle).

Repeat last row until strap measures 24 inches (61 cm) or until desired length to match the right strap. Bind off.

## BACK STRAPS

### Right Side Strap

With the RS facing you and using US 4 (3.5 mm) needles, beginning at the left removable stm, pick up and k2. Remove marker.

**Next row:** K2. Slide sts to end of needle (or transfer back to left needle).

Repeat last row until strap measures 26 (27, 28, 29, 30) (31, 32, 33, 34, 35)" / 66 (69, 71, 74, 76) (79, 81, 84, 86, 89) cm or until desired length. Bind off.

### Left Side Strap

With the RS facing you and using US 4 (3.5 mm) needles, beginning at the right removable stm, pick up and k2. Remove marker.

**Next row:** K2. Slide sts to end of needle (or transfer back to left needle).

Repeat last row until strap measures 26 (27, 28, 29, 30) (31, 32, 33, 34, 35)" / 66 (69, 71, 74, 76) (79, 81, 84, 86, 89) cm or until desired length to match the right strap. Bind off.

## FINISHING

Weave in any loose ends. Block your project using your preferred method.

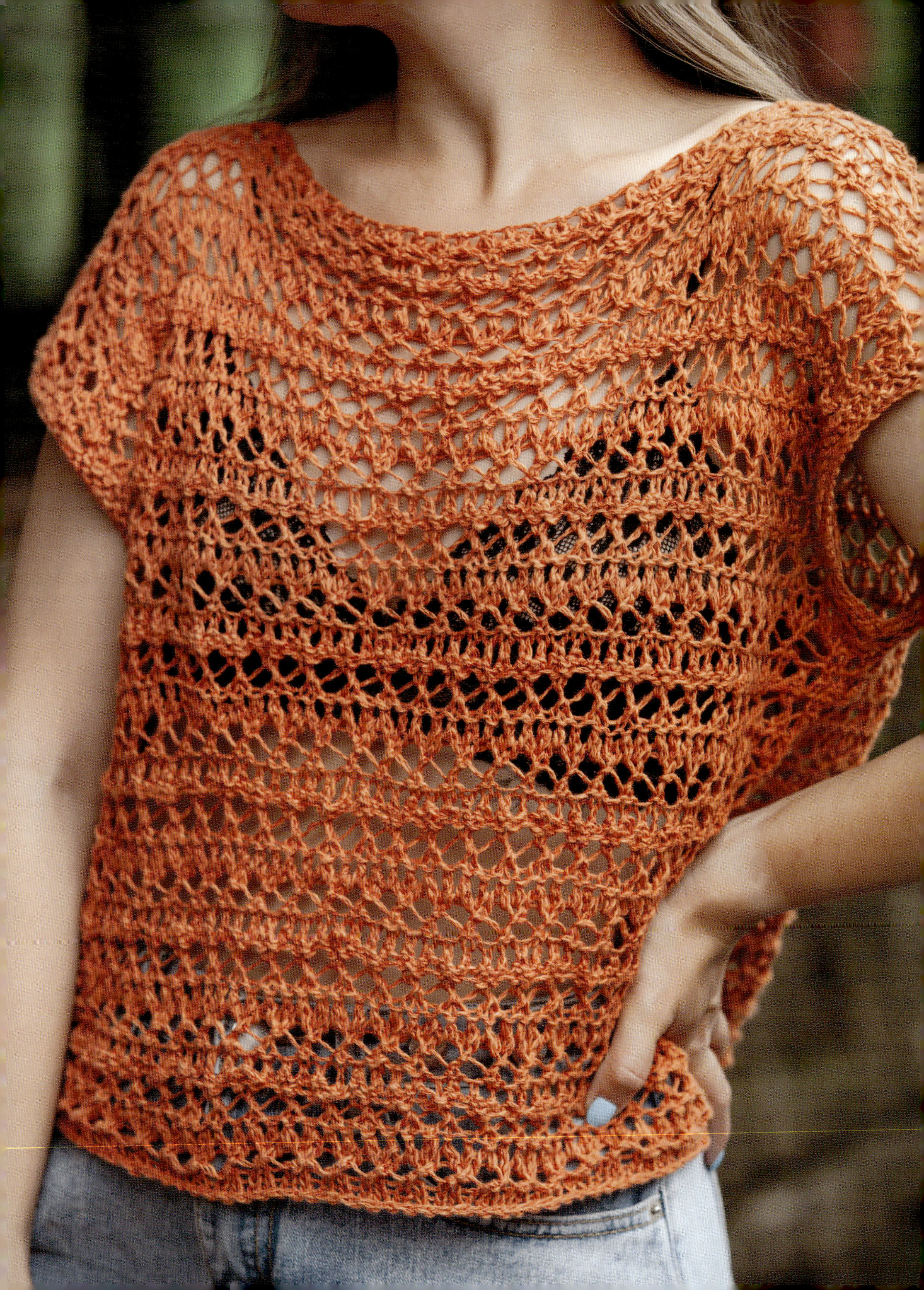

# Hollyberry Tee

Every knitter needs a comfy tee in their wardrobe, and the Hollyberry Tee checks all the boxes. The combination of openwork lace in a modern, boxy shape creates a drapey fabric that allows the wearer to feel both comfortable and stylish on the sunniest of days.

Incorporating knit and purl stitches with yarnovers and decreases, the result is an elongated stitch pattern that is visually striking yet deceptively simple to knit. The construction of the garment is also straightforward, consisting of two identical panels that are seamed together, making the project suitable for knitters of all levels.

A cotton and linen blend yarn was chosen for the sample in order to create a strong but drapey fabric with a hint of sheen, but any plant-based fiber would be an excellent choice for this project. With a boxy tee, the outfit options are endless: You can wear it with your favorite bralette and skirt for date night, or create a contrast by pairing it with slim-fit pants.

## Construction Notes

*The tee consists of two identical rectangular panels, worked flat from the top down (although this can be flipped depending on your preference of how the stitches look). Once both pieces are completed, the shoulders and sides are seamed. Stitches are picked up for the armholes and worked in the round to create a sleeve edge.*

## SKILL LEVEL
*Advanced Beginner*

## SIZING
XS (S, M, L, XL) (2XL, 3XL, 4XL, 5XL, 6XL)

Bust circumference of 33.75 (37.5, 41.25, 46.25, 51) (54.75, 59.75, 63.5, 68.25, 70.75)" / 86 (95, 105, 117, 130) (139, 152, 161, 174, 180) cm, blocked

## Materials

### Yarn
Sport weight, Juniper Moon Farm Zooey in Caramel (60% cotton, 40% linen), 284 yds (260 m) per 100-g skein

Any sport to DK weight yarn can be used for this pattern as long as it matches gauge.

### Yardage/Meterage
450 (460, 505, 640, 715) (710, 815, 865, 930, 965) yds / 410 (420, 460, 585, 650) (645, 745, 790, 850, 880) m of sport weight yarn

### Needles
**For body:** US 8 (5 mm) straight or circular needles

**For sleeve finishing:** US 8 (5 mm), 16- to 24-inch (40- to 60-cm) circular or double pointed needles

### Notions
Stitch marker

Tapestry needle

## GAUGE
13 sts x 24.25 rows = 4 inches (10 cm) in Roman Stripe Stitch worked flat (blocked and stretched)

## TECHNIQUES

*Horizontal Invisible Seam (page 149)*

*Mattress Stitch (page 150)*

*Roman Stripe Stitch (Multiples of 2)*

**Row 1:** *K1, \*k1, yo; rep from \* until last st, k1.*

**Row 2:** *K1, p until last st, k1.*

**Row 3:** *K1, \*k2tog; rep from \* until last st, k1.*

**Row 4:** *K1, \*k2tog, yo; rep from \* until last st, k1.*

**Row 5:** *K1, \*yo, k2tog; rep from \* until last st, k1.*

**Rows 6–7:** *K all sts.*

**NOTE:** *Due to the increases in row 1, there will be double the number of sts in rows 1 & 2. Rows 3–7 will return to the original number of cast on sts.*

## ABBREVIATIONS

| | |
|---|---|
| DPN(s) | double pointed needle(s) |
| k | knit |
| k2tog | knit 2 sts together [1 st decreased] |
| p | purl |
| pm | place marker |
| rep | repeat |
| RS | right side |
| st(s) | stitch(es) |
| WS | wrong side |
| yo | yarnover |

## SIZING CHART

| | XS | S | M | L | XL | 2XL | 3XL | 4XL | 5XL | 6XL | |
|---|---|---|---|---|---|---|---|---|---|---|---|
| A) Body Circumference | 33.75 | 37.5 | 41.25 | 46.25 | 51 | 54.75 | 59.75 | 63.5 | 68.25 | 70.75 | in |
| | 86 | 95 | 105 | 117 | 130 | 139 | 152 | 161 | 174 | 180 | cm |
| B) Shoulder Width | 12 | 13.75 | 15.5 | 18 | 20.5 | 22.5 | 24.75 | 26.75 | 29.25 | 30.5 | in |
| | 30 | 35 | 40 | 46 | 52 | 57 | 63 | 68 | 74 | 77 | cm |
| C) Armhole Depth | 7.5 | 8 | 8.5 | 9 | 9.5 | 10 | 10.5 | 11 | 11.5 | 12 | in |
| | 19 | 20 | 22 | 23 | 24 | 26 | 27 | 28 | 29 | 31 | cm |
| D) Garment Length | 17.5 | 17.5 | 17.5 | 18.75 | 18.75 | 18.75 | 19.75 | 19.75 | 19.75 | 19.75 | in |
| | 45 | 45 | 45 | 47 | 47 | 47 | 50 | 50 | 50 | 50 | cm |

The top is designed with 4 to 8 inches (10 to 20 cm) of positive ease. Sample shown is knit in size S. If in between sizes, it is recommended to select the smaller size.

## SCHEMATIC

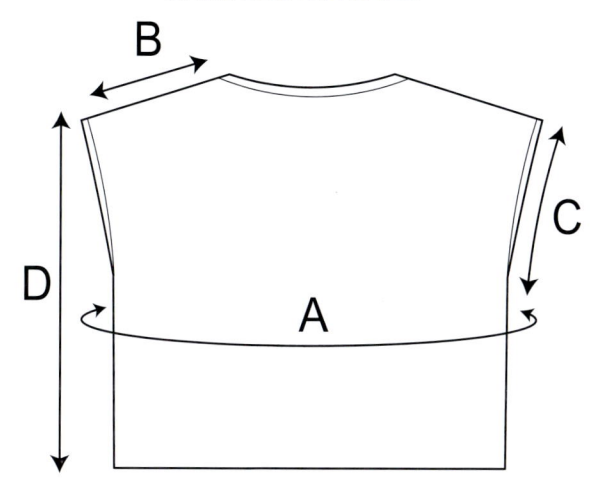

Festival & Beach Knits

# HOLLYBERRY TEE PATTERN

## BODY (MAKE 2)
Using US 8 (5 mm) needles, cast on 56 (62, 68, 76, 84) (90, 98, 104, 112, 116) sts using the longtail cast on method.

> **TIP:** *If you leave a long tail prior to cast on and at bind off, you won't need additional yarn for seaming the sides and the shoulders later. The recommended amount is double the length of the side, or approximately 14 (17.5, 21, 26, 31) (35, 39.5, 43.5, 48.5, 51)" / 36 (45, 53, 66, 79) (89, 100, 111, 123, 130) cm.*

**Row 1 (RS):** K1, *k1, yo; rep from * until last st, k1. [110 (122, 134, 150, 166) (178, 194, 206, 222, 230) sts]—The total number of sts have been doubled.

**Row 2 (WS):** K1, p until last st, k1. [110 (122, 134, 150, 166) (178, 194, 206, 222, 230) sts]

**Row 3:** K1, *k2tog; rep from * until last st, k1. [56 (62, 68, 76, 84) (90, 98, 104, 112, 116) sts]—The total number of sts has been halved.

**Row 4:** K1, *k2tog, yo; rep from * until last st, k1. [56 (62, 68, 76, 84) (90, 98, 104, 112, 116) sts]

**Row 5:** K1, *yo, k2tog; rep from * until last st, k1. [56 (62, 68, 76, 84) (90, 98, 104, 112, 116) sts]

**Rows 6–7:** K all sts. [56 (62, 68, 76, 84) (90, 98, 104, 112, 116) sts]

Repeat rows 1–7 a total of 13 more times.

> **NOTE:** *Since the stitch pattern is repeated in sets of 7 rows, the RS of your piece will alternate with each repeat.*

Repeat rows 1–5.

**Next row (WS):** K1, p all until last st, k1.

**Next row (RS):** K all sts.

**Next row:** K1, p all until last st, k1.

Bind off all sts knitwise loosely.

> **NOTE:** *This stitch pattern has an odd row count, which means that rows 1 & 2 have a different stitch count than rows 3–7. This means that prior to blocking, your piece will likely have jagged sides. This is normal and I recommend wet blocking prior to seaming the shoulders and sides.*

## Seaming the Shoulders

Wet block your garment. Once the garment has finished drying and with the RSs facing out, beginning from the outside edge use a tapestry needle and the horizontal invisible seaming method to seam the shoulders for 3.5 (4.5, 5.25, 6.5, 7.75) (8.75, 10, 10.75, 12, 12.75)" / 9 (11, 13, 17, 20) (22, 25, 28, 31, 32) cm in length on each side, starting from the outer edges. This will leave a 10-inch (25-cm) neck opening. Feel free to adjust if you want a smaller or bigger opening.

## Seaming the Sides

Starting at the bottom, use a tapestry needle and the mattress st to seam the sides for 10 (9.5, 9, 9.75, 9.25) (8.75, 9.25, 8.75, 8.25, 7.75)" / 25 (24, 23, 25, 23) (22, 23, 22, 21, 20) cm, leaving a 7.5 (8, 8.5, 9, 9.5) (10, 10.5, 11, 11.5, 12)" / 19 (20, 22, 23, 24) (26, 27, 28, 29, 31) cm sleeve opening.

## SLEEVE EDGE (MAKE 2)

Using US 8 (5 mm) circular needles or DPNs and beginning with the center of the underarm, evenly pick up and k30 (32, 34, 36, 38) (40, 42, 44, 46, 48) towards the shoulder, then evenly pick up and k30 (32, 34, 36, 38) (40, 42, 44, 46, 48) back towards the underarm. Pm and join for working in the round. [60 (64, 68, 72, 76) (80, 84, 88, 92, 96) sts]

**Round 1:** P all sts.

**Round 2:** K all sts.

**Round 3:** P all sts.

Bind off all sts knitwise.

## FINISHING

Weave in any loose ends. Feel free to re-block your garment after seaming, although this is not necessary.

Festival & Beach Knits

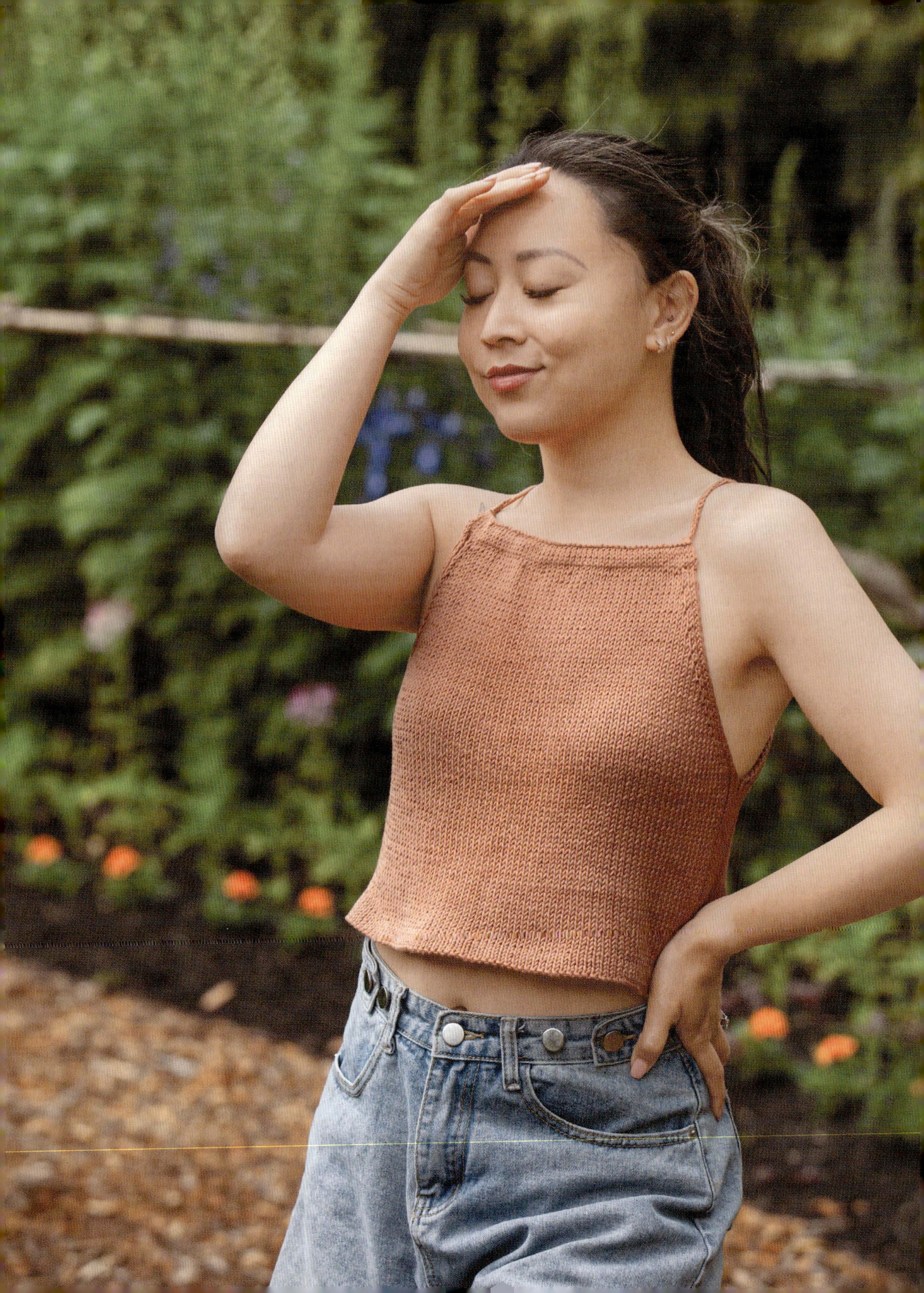

# Knits for Any Occasion

## Versatile Tops to Dress Up or Down

When I first started building my handknit wardrobe, it was important to include pieces that could easily be paired with other articles of clothing or worn across various occasions. Since I was going to invest so much time and materials in these handmade garments, I wanted to ensure they got as much wear as possible. The beauty in the final three patterns of this book is that you can mix and match so many different outfits to be worn in multiple settings. While versatility is truly the name of the game, these designs are far from basic or ordinary.

Pair the Plume Halter (page 121) with your favorite pair of barrel pants for a casual, laid-back look or wear it with cargo pants for a sportier ensemble. The thick, almost ribbon-like halter ties add a feminine detail to any outfit and the cropped length make it a good fit for all types of bottoms. Similarly, the Hibiscus Top (page 127) would look equally cute with a matching skirt or denim shorts due to its simple lines, stitchwork and structure. Lastly, the Camellia Wrap Top (page 135) can be easily dressed up or down depending on your choice of footwear and outerwear. The I-cord ties can be wrapped around your bare waist for a flirty look or layered over another top for a more modest occasion.

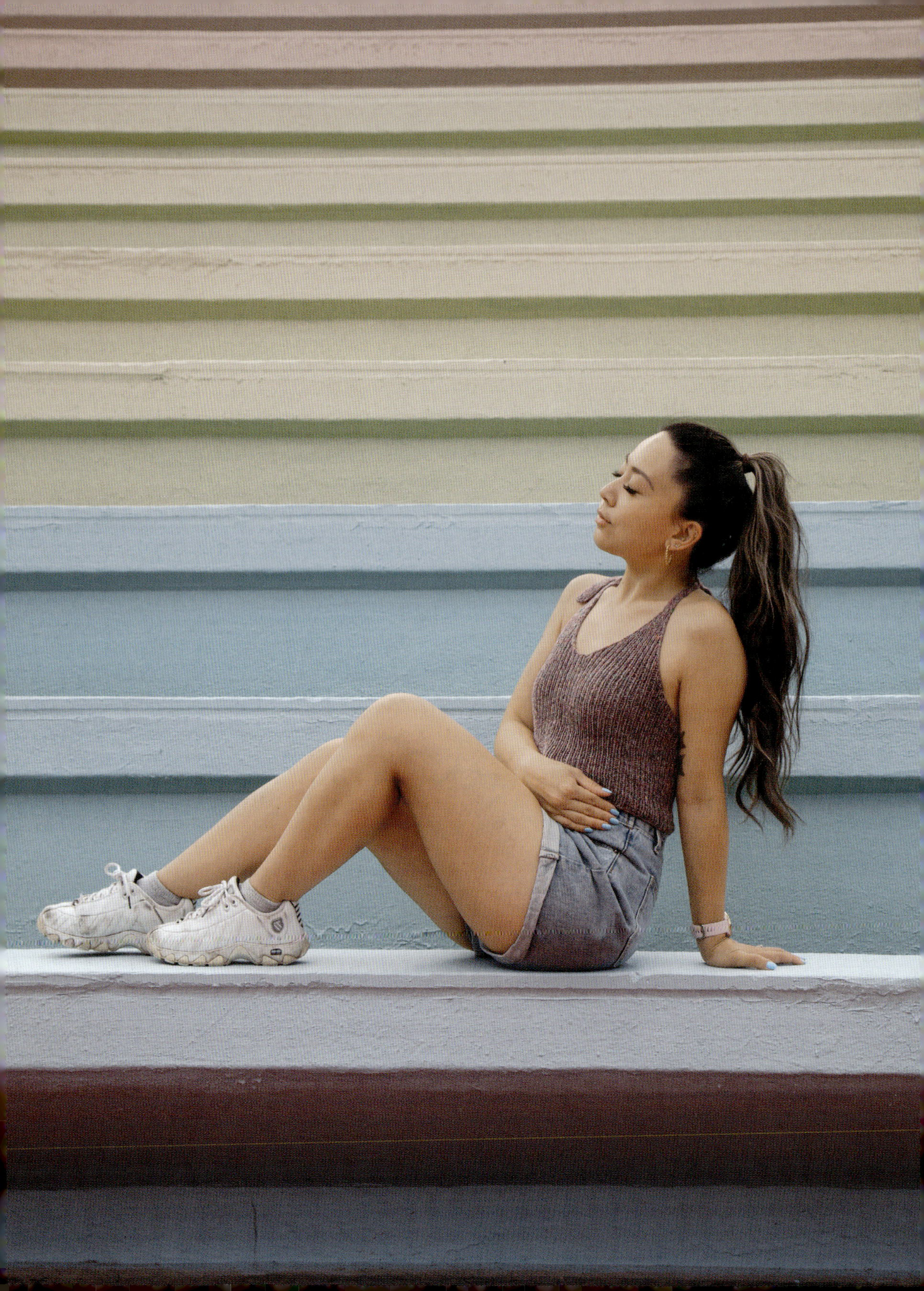

# Plume Halter

Hop on the continued Y2K trend with your very own handknit halter! With ribbon-like straps that tie like a bow at the nape of your neck, the Plume Halter is a modern take on a classic silhouette. Cropped and ribbed throughout, the stretchy fabric creates a body-hugging fit that will complement both high and low-rise bottoms. The straps allow you to adjust for your desired bust coverage, and the tapered ends add a decorative feature that is also practical. The straps can also be worn crisscrossed in the front before tying behind your neck. Now the question remains: Will you be going all out '90s with cargo pants and butterfly clips, or will you be staying in the current decade?

## Construction Notes

*The halter is worked in the round from the bottom up. Once the length of the body is reached, stitches are bound off for the back. The right front cup is worked flat in continuous decreases until it becomes the width of the strap. The right front strap is then knit in double stockinette stitch until it is long enough to be tied into a bow, and then a staggered bind off is worked to create a tapered edge. The same process is then repeated for the left front cup and strap.*

## SKILL LEVEL
*Advanced Beginner*

## SIZING
XS (S, M, L, XL) (2XL, 3XL, 4XL, 5XL, 6XL)

Bust circumference of 29.5 (33.5, 37.5, 41.5, 45.5) (49.5, 53.5, 57.5, 61.5, 65.5)" / 75 (85, 96, 106, 116) (126, 136, 146, 157, 167) cm, blocked

## Materials

### Yarn
DK weight, Rowan Purelife Revive in 00472 Loam (36% recycled silk, 36% recycled cotton, 28% recycled viscose), 137 yds (125 m) per 50-g skein

Any DK weight yarn can be used for this pattern as long as it matches gauge.

## Yardage/Meterage
270 (310, 345, 390, 435) (485, 535, 595, 655, 690) yds / 245 (280, 315, 355, 395) (440, 490, 540, 595, 630) m of DK weight yarn

## Needles
**For straps:** US 4 (3.5 mm) straight or double pointed needles

**For body:** US 6 (4 mm), 24- to 60-inch (60- to 150-cm) circular needles

## Notions
Scrap yarn or stitch holder

Stitch markers

Tapestry needle

## GAUGE
20 sts x 31 rounds = 4 inches (10 cm) in 1x1 ribbing using larger needles (blocked and stretched)

**NOTE:** *It is difficult to measure gauge accurately when it comes to ribbing due to the amount of stretch. If you are able to get close to gauge stretched OR unstretched, the garment will fit.*

## TECHNIQUES
Double Stockinette Stitch (page 153)

# ABBREVIATIONS

| | |
|---|---|
| BOR | beginning of round |
| k | knit |
| k2tog | knit 2 sts together [1 st decreased] |
| p | purl |
| patt | pattern |
| pm | place marker |
| rem | remain(ing) |
| rep | repeat |
| RS | right side |
| sl1wyif | slip 1 st purlwise with yarn in front |
| ssk | slip 2 sts knitwise, one at a time; move both stitches back to the left needle; knit these 2 sts together through the back loops [1 st decreased] |
| st(s) | stitch(es) |
| stm(s) | stitch marker(s) |
| WS | wrong side |

## SIZING CHART

|  | XS | S | M | L | XL | 2XL | 3XL | 4XL | 5XL | 6XL |  |
|---|---|---|---|---|---|---|---|---|---|---|---|
| A) Body Circumference | 29.5 | 33.5 | 37.5 | 41.5 | 45.5 | 49.5 | 53.5 | 57.5 | 61.5 | 65.5 | in |
|  | 75 | 85 | 96 | 106 | 116 | 126 | 136 | 146 | 157 | 167 | cm |
| B) Cup Height | 3.5 | 4.25 | 4.75 | 5.25 | 6 | 6.5 | 7 | 7.75 | 8.25 | 8.75 | in |
|  | 9 | 11 | 12 | 13 | 15 | 17 | 18 | 20 | 21 | 22 | cm |
| C) Garment Length | 11.5 | 12.75 | 13.75 | 14.75 | 16 | 17 | 18 | 19.25 | 20.25 | 21.25 | in |
|  | 29 | 33 | 35 | 38 | 41 | 43 | 46 | 49 | 52 | 54 | cm |

*The top is designed with -4 to -2 inches (-10 to -5 cm) of negative ease. Sample shown is knit in size XS.*

## SCHEMATIC

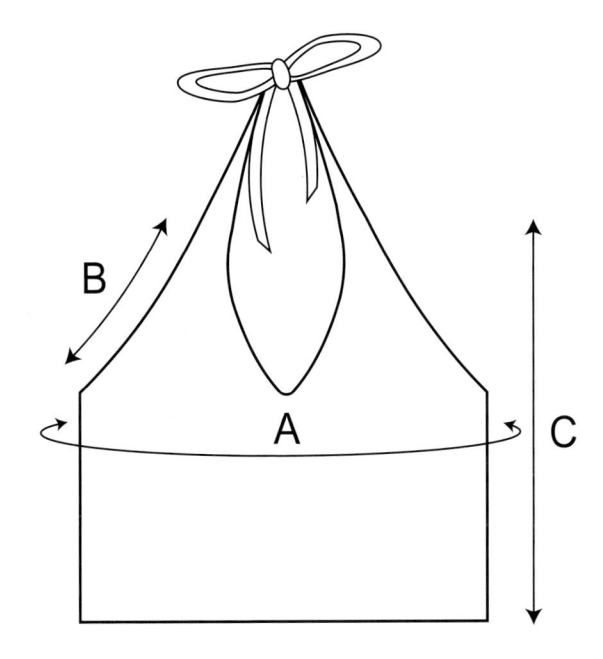

Knits for Any Occasion

# PLUME HALTER PATTERN

## BODY

Using US 6 (4 mm) needles, cast on 148 (168, 188, 208, 228) (248, 268, 288, 308, 328) sts using the longtail cast on method. Pm and join for working in the round.

**Round 1:** *K1, p1; rep from * until end.

Repeat last row until piece measures 8 (8.5, 9, 9.5, 10) (10.5, 11, 11.5, 12, 12.5)" / 20 (22, 23, 24, 25) (27, 28, 29, 30, 32) cm.

## Bind Off Back

**Next row (RS):** Remove BOR stm. Bind off 74 (84, 94, 104, 114) (124, 134, 144, 154, 164) sts, work 35 (40, 45, 49, 54) (59, 63, 68, 72, 77) sts in patt, bind off 4 (4, 4, 6, 6) (6, 8, 8, 10, 10) sts, work rem sts in patt until the last st, sl1wyif. Leave rem 35 (40, 45, 49, 54) (59, 63, 68, 72, 77) sts for the left front on a holder or spare yarn to return to later.

## FRONT RIGHT

**Next row (WS):** Work sts in patt until last st, sl1wyif.

**Next row (RS):** K1, ssk, work in patt until last 3 sts, k2tog, sl1wyif. [33 (38, 43, 47, 52) (57, 61, 66, 70, 75) sts rem, 2 sts decreased]

**Next row:** K1, p1, work in patt until last 2 sts, p1, sl1wyif.

Repeat last 2 rows a total of 12 (15, 17, 19, 22) (24, 26, 29, 31, 33) more times until 9 (8, 9, 9, 8) (9, 9, 8, 8, 9) sts rem.

*Sizes XS, M, L, 2XL, 3XL & 6XL only*

**Next row (RS):** K1, ssk, (k1, sl1wyif) 3 times. [8 sts rem]

**Next row:** K1, p1, work in patt until last 2 sts, p1, sl1wyif.

*All sizes resume*

## RIGHT STRAP

Switch to US 4 (3.5 mm) needles.

**Next row (RS):** *K1, sl1wyif; rep from * until end.

Repeat last row until strap measures 20 inches (51 cm). Your last row should be a WS row.

**Next row (RS):** Slip first 2 sts purlwise to the right needle one by one. Slip first st over second st to bind off 1 st. Bind off the next st normally, sl1wyif, (k1, sl1wyif) twice. [6 sts rem]

**Next row (WS):** *K1, sl1wyif; rep from * 2 times.

**Next row:** Slip first 2 sts purlwise to the right needle one by one. Slip first st over second st to bind off 1 st. Bind off the next st normally, sl1wyif, k1, sl1wyif. [4 sts rem]

**Next row:** *K1, sl1wyif; rep from * 1 time.

**Next row:** Slip first 2 sts purlwise to the right needle one by one. Slip first st over second st to bind off 1 st. Bind off the next st normally, sl1wyif. [2 sts rem]

**Next row:** K1, sl1wyif.

**Next row:** Slip both rem sts purlwise to the right needle one by one. Slip first st over second st to bind off 1 st. Tie off last st, and weave in the loose end.

## FRONT LEFT

Rejoin yarn to WS of work using US 6 (4 mm) needles.

**Next row (WS):** Work in patt until last st, sl1wyif.

**Next row (RS):** K1, ssk, work in patt until last 3 sts, k2tog, sl1wyif. [33 (38, 43, 47, 52) (57, 61, 66, 70, 75) sts rem, 2 sts decreased]

**Next row:** K1, p1, work in patt until last 2 sts, p1, sl1wyif.

Repeat last 2 rows a total of 12 (15, 17, 19, 22) (24, 26, 29, 31, 33) more times until 9 (8, 9, 9, 8) (9, 9, 8, 8, 9) sts rem.

*Sizes XS, M, L, 2XL, 3XL & 6XL only*
**Next row (RS):** K1, ssk, (k1, sl1wyif) 3 times. [8 sts rem]

**Next row (WS):** K1, p1, work in patt until last 2 sts, p1, sl1wyif.

*All sizes resume*

## LEFT STRAP

Switch to US 4 (3.5 mm) needles.

**Next row (RS):** *K1, sl1wyif; rep from * until end.

Repeat last row until strap measures 20 inches (51 cm). Your last row should be a RS row in order to mirror the other strap.

**Next row (WS):** Slip first 2 sts purlwise to the right needle one by one. Slip first st over second st to bind off 1 st. Bind off the next st normally, sl1wyif, (k1, sl1wyif) twice. [6 sts rem]

**Next row (RS):** *K1, sl1wyif; rep from * 2 times.

**Next row:** Slip first 2 sts purlwise to the right needle one by one. Slip first st over second st to bind off 1 st. Bind off the next st normally, sl1wyif, k1, sl1wyif. [4 sts rem]

**Next row:** *K1, sl1wyif; rep from * 1 time.

**Next row:** Slip first 2 sts purlwise to the right needle one by one. Slip first st over second st to bind off 1 st. Bind off the next st normally, sl1wyif. [2 sts rem]

**Next row:** K1, sl1wyif.

**Next row:** Slip both rem sts purlwise to the right needle one by one. Slip first st over second st to bind off 1 st. Tie off last st, and weave in the loose end.

## FINISHING

Weave in any loose ends. Block your project using your preferred method.

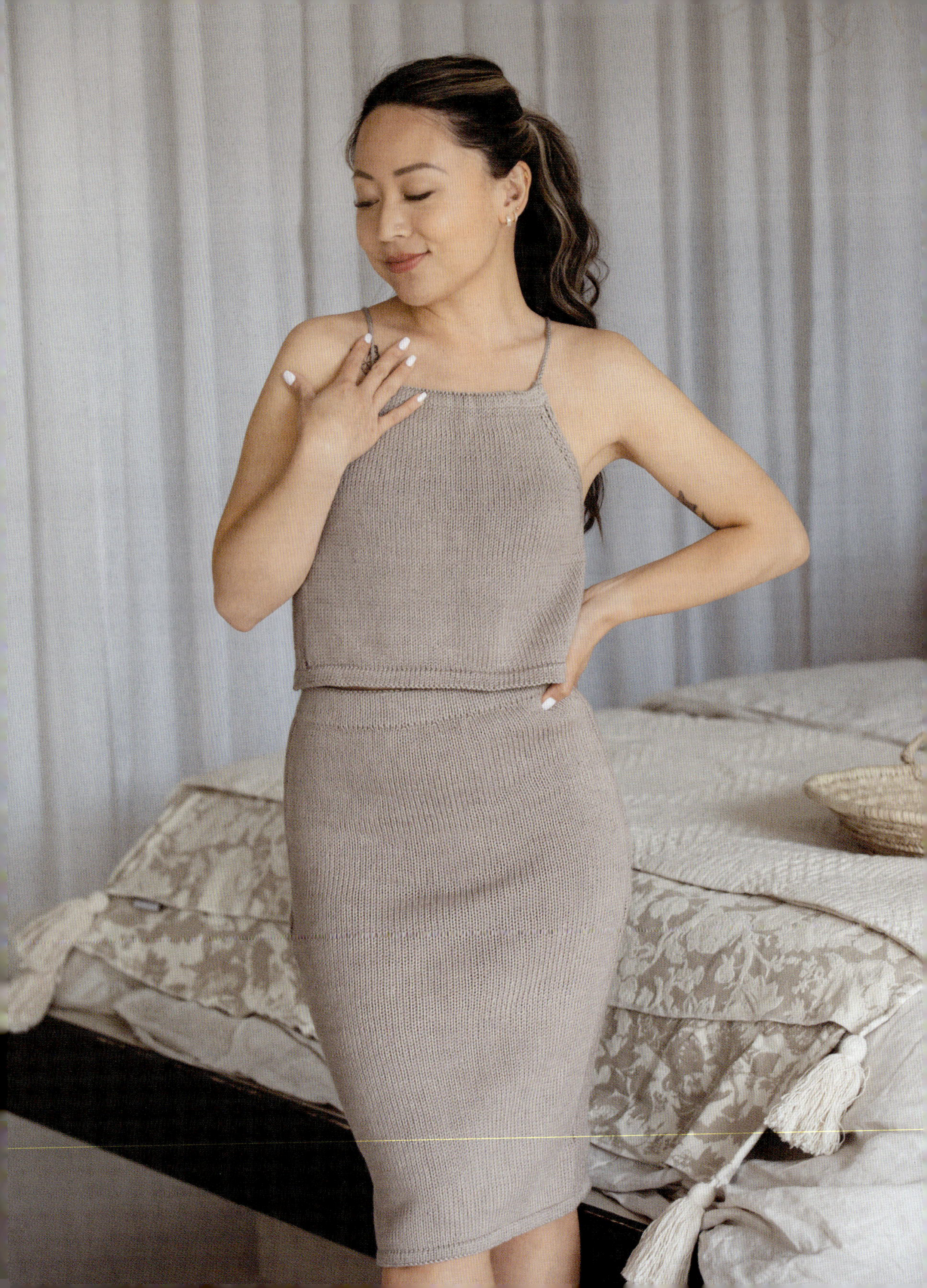

# Hibiscus Top

The Hibiscus Top is once again another versatile piece to add to your summer knits collection. With adjustable straps to help you achieve the perfect fit, the top can be worn low and loose with a bralette underneath or higher on the neck if you prefer a halter-style fit. The front hem can also be worn gathered at the neckline since the strap can create a ruched drawstring effect. You can even wear the top backwards with the fastening in the front, as I've done on several occasions.

Whether styled with a pair of denim shorts or worn with another knit skirt for a chic ensemble, you can seamlessly transition your outfit from day to night. By just swapping out your bottoms, adding in some accessories or draping a blazer over your shoulders, the Hibiscus Top can also work in both casual and professional settings.

## Construction Notes

*The top is worked from the top down, beginning with the back right piece that is worked flat and then set aside. You will then cast on for the back left, which mirrors the back right piece. These two pieces are joined to form the back and increases are made until the desired width is achieved. The piece is set aside once again.*

*Next, you will cast on for the front and increases are worked until the desired bust width is achieved. The front piece is then joined with the previously set aside back piece and you will continue working the rest of the body in the round, ending with a folded hem. Finally, an I-cord strap is knit and inserted into the back left, front and back right hems and the ends are fastened into a bow.*

## SKILL LEVEL
*Advanced Beginner*

## SIZING
XS (S, M, L, XL) (2XL, 3XL, 4XL, 5XL, 6XL)

Bust circumference of 30.25 (34, 38.5, 42.25, 47) (50, 54.5, 58.25, 62.25, 66)" / 77 (86, 98, 108, 119) (127, 139, 148, 158, 168) cm, blocked

## Materials

### Yarn
Worsted weight, We Are Knitters The Cotton in Pearl Gray (100% cotton), 232 yds (212 m) per 100-g skein

An alternate sample was knit with We Are Knitters The Cotton in Canyon Rose.

Any worsted weight yarn can be used for this pattern as long as it matches gauge. Alternatively, a DK weight yarn can also be used if you prefer a top with additional drape.

### Yardage/Meterage
390 (475, 520, 560, 600) (730, 865, 970, 1100, 1260) yds / 360 (435, 475, 515, 550) (670, 795, 890, 1010, 1155) m of worsted (or DK) weight yarn

### Needles
**For folded hem:** US 4 (3.5 mm), 16- to 40-inch (40- to 100-cm) circular needles

**For top:** US 6 (4 mm), 24- to 60-inch (60- to 150-cm) circular needles

**For straps:** US 4 (3.5 mm) straight or double pointed needles

### Notions
Safety pin

Scissors

Scrap yarn in a contrasting color

Stitch markers

Tapestry needle

## GAUGE

*21 sts x 29 rounds = 4 inches (10 cm) in stockinette st using larger needles (blocked)*

*32 sts x 29 rounds = 4 inches (10 cm) in 1x1 twisted rib using larger needles (blocked)*

## TECHNIQUES

*Backwards Loop Cast On (page 142)*

*I-Cord (page 153)*

*Whip Stitch (page 150)*

# ABBREVIATIONS

| | |
|---|---|
| 1x1 twisted rib(bing) | *k1tbl, p1tbl; repeat from * until end |
| BOR | beginning of round |
| inc | increase |
| k | knit |
| k1tbl | knit through the back loop |
| m1l | make 1 left: use the left needle to pick up the strand between the last worked st and the next unworked st from front to back, knit this st through the back loop [1 st increased] |
| p | purl |
| p1tbl | purl through the back loop |
| pm | place marker |
| RLI | right lifted increase: identify the st one row below the next st on your left needle; insert the right needle tip into the right leg of this st from back to front and lift this strand onto the left needle; knit into this st |
| RS | right side |
| sl1wyib | slip 1 st purlwise with yarn in back |
| sl1wyif | slip 1 st purlwise with yarn in front |
| sm | slip marker |
| st(s) | stitch(es) |
| stm | stitch marker |
| WS | wrong side |

Light & Breezy Knitwear

## SIZING CHART

|  | XS | S | M | L | XL | 2XL | 3XL | 4XL | 5XL | 6XL |  |
|---|---|---|---|---|---|---|---|---|---|---|---|
| A) Body Circumference | 30.25 | 34 | 38.5 | 42.25 | 47 | 50 | 54.5 | 58.25 | 62.25 | 66 | in |
|  | 77 | 86 | 98 | 108 | 119 | 127 | 139 | 148 | 158 | 168 | cm |
| B) Armhole Length for Back Piece | 6.25 | 6.5 | 8 | 8.5 | 9 | 9.5 | 10 | 10.75 | 11.25 | 11.75 | in |
|  | 16 | 17 | 20 | 22 | 23 | 24 | 26 | 27 | 29 | 30 | cm |
| C) Body Length from Underarm | 7 | 7 | 8 | 8 | 8 | 8 | 9 | 9 | 9 | 9 | in |
|  | 18 | 18 | 20 | 20 | 20 | 20 | 23 | 23 | 23 | 23 | cm |
| D) Garment Length | 13.25 | 13.8 | 16 | 16.3 | 17 | 17.8 | 19 | 19.50 | 20.25 | 21 | in |
|  | 34 | 35 | 39 | 41 | 43 | 45 | 47 | 49 | 51 | 53 | cm |

*The top is designed with 0 to 3 inches (0 to 8 cm) of neutral to positive ease. Sample shown is knit in size XS.*

## SCHEMATIC

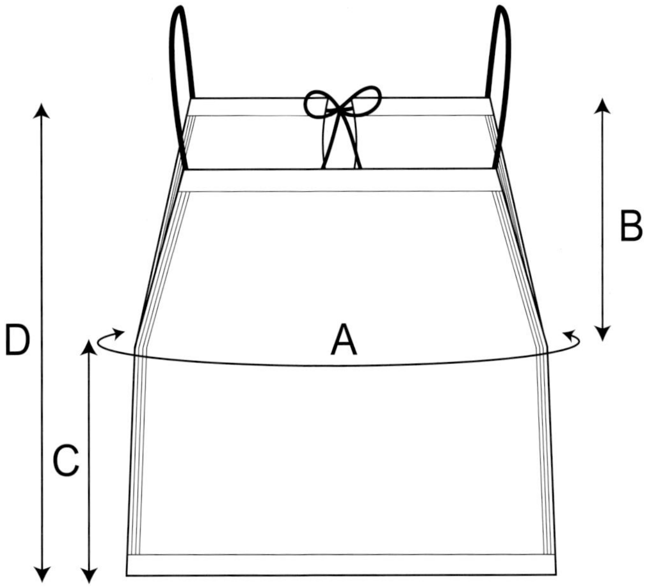

Knits for Any Occasion

Row 7: P all sts.

Row 8: Fold your work so the purl row is now the bottom edge. Pick up the corresponding st from the cast on edge and place on left needle. K it together with the st from the current round. Repeat until end.

Row 9: P all sts.

Switch to US 6 (4 mm) needles.

Row 1 (RS): Sl1wyib, k until last 5 sts, k1tbl, (p1tbl, k1tbl) twice.

Row 2 (WS): Sl1wyif, (k1tbl, p1tbl) twice, p until end.

Row 3: Sl1wyib, k until last 5 sts, m1l, k1tbl, (p1tbl, k1tbl) twice. [24 (28, 30, 32, 36) (38, 42, 44, 48, 52) sts, 1 st increased]

Row 4: Sl1wyif, (k1tbl, p1tbl) twice, p until end.

Repeat rows 1–4 a total of 6 (7, 7, 8, 10) (11, 12, 13, 14, 14) more times until you have 30 (35, 37, 40, 46) (49, 54, 57, 62, 66) sts. Break yarn and set aside.

## BACK LEFT TOP HEM
Using US 4 (3.5 mm) needles, cast on 23 (27, 29, 31, 35) (37, 41, 43, 47, 51) sts using the longtail cast on method.

Row 1 (WS): P all sts.

Row 2 (RS): K all sts.

Row 3: P all sts.

Row 4 (RS, turning row): P all sts.

Row 5: P all sts.

Row 6: K all sts.

# HIBISCUS TOP PATTERN

## BACK RIGHT TOP HEM
Using US 4 (3.5 mm) needles, cast on 23 (27, 29, 31, 35) (37, 41, 43, 47, 51) sts using the longtail cast on method.

Row 1 (WS): P all sts.

Row 2 (RS): K all sts.

Row 3: P all sts.

Row 4 (RS, turning row): P all sts.

Row 5: P all sts.

Row 6: K all sts.

**Row 7:** P all sts.

**Row 8:** Fold your work so the purl row is now the bottom edge. Pick up the corresponding st from the cast on edge and place on left needle. K it together with the st from the current round. Repeat until end.

**Row 9:** P all sts.

Switch to US 6 (4 mm) needles.

**Row 1 (RS):** Sl1wyib, (p1tbl, k1tbl) twice, k until end.

**Row 2 (WS):** Sl1wyif, p until last 5 sts, p1tbl, (k1tbl, p1tbl) twice.

**Row 3:** Sl1wyib, (p1tbl, k1tbl) twice, RLI, k until end. [24 (28, 30, 32, 36) (38, 42, 44, 48, 52) sts, 1 st increased]

**Row 4:** Sl1wyif, p until last 5 sts, p1tbl, (k1tbl, p1tbl) twice.

Repeat rows 1–4 a total of 6 (7, 7, 8, 10) (11, 12, 13, 14, 14) more times until you have 30 (35, 37, 40, 46) (49, 54, 57, 62, 66) sts.

*DESIGNER'S NOTE: You may notice that the techniques for increases on the left (m1l) and right (RLI) side of the garment are different. After much trial and error, I found that these two techniques were the most visually appealing for this design when increases are worked from the top down next to twisted stitches.*

## Join Back Right/Left

**Next row (RS):** Sl1wyib, (p1tbl, k1tbl) twice, k until end. Take the previously set aside sts from the back right piece and work them on the RS as follows: K until last 5 sts, k1tbl, (p1tbl, k1tbl) twice. [60 (70, 74, 80, 92) (98, 108, 114, 124, 132) sts]

**Next row (WS):** Sl1wyif, (k1tbl, p1tbl) twice, p until last 5 sts, p1tbl, (k1tbl, p1tbl) twice.

**Next row (RS, inc):** Sl1wyib, (p1tbl, k1tbl) twice, RLI, k until last 5 sts, m1l, k1tbl, (p1tbl, k1tbl) twice. [62 (72, 76, 82, 94) (100, 110, 116, 126, 134), 2 sts increased]

Repeat last 2 rows a total of 10 (10, 14, 16, 16) (17, 18, 20, 20, 21) more times until you have 82 (92, 104, 114, 126) (134, 146, 156, 166, 176) sts. Repeat a WS row one more time. Break yarn and set aside.

## FRONT TOP HEM

Using US 4 (3.5 mm) needles, cast on 52 (60, 64, 70, 80) (84, 94, 100, 108, 114) sts using the longtail cast on method.

**Row 1 (WS):** P all sts.

**Row 2 (RS):** K all sts.

**Row 3:** P all sts.

**Row 4 (RS, turning row):** P all sts.

**Row 5:** P all sts.

**Row 6:** K all sts.

**Row 7:** P all sts.

**Row 8:** Fold your work so the purl row is now the bottom edge. Pick up the corresponding st from the cast on edge and place on left needle. K it together with the st from the current round. Repeat until end.

**Row 9:** P all sts.

Switch to US 6 (4 mm) needles.

**Row 1 (RS):** Sl1wyib, (p1tbl, k1tbl) twice, k until last 5 sts, k1tbl, (p1tbl, k1tbl) twice.

**Row 2 (WS):** Sl1wyif, (k1tbl, p1tbl) twice, p until last 5 sts, p1tbl, (k1tbl, p1tbl) twice.

**Row 3:** Sl1wyib, (p1tbl, k1tbl) twice, RLI, k until last 5 sts, m1l, k1tbl, (p1tbl, k1tbl) twice. [54 (62, 66, 72, 82) (86, 96, 102, 110, 116) sts, 2 sts increased]

**Row 4:** Sl1wyif, (k1tbl, p1tbl) twice, p until last 5 sts, p1tbl, (k1tbl, p1tbl) twice.

Repeat rows 1–4 a total of 4 (4, 5, 5, 6) (6, 7, 7, 8, 8) more times until you have 62 (70, 76, 82, 94) (98, 110, 116, 126, 132) sts.

Repeat rows 3–4 a total of 10 (11, 14, 16, 16) (18, 18, 20, 20, 22) more times until you have 82 (92, 104, 114, 126) (134, 146, 156, 166, 176) sts.

## Join Front/Back

**Set-up round:** K1tbl, (p1tbl, k1tbl) twice, k until last 5 sts, k1tbl, (p1tbl, k1tbl) twice, loosely cast on 1 st using the backwards loop method, pm for side. You will now be working across the RS of the back piece as follows: K1tbl, (p1tbl, k1tbl) twice, k until last 5 sts, k1tbl, (p1tbl, k1tbl) twice, loosely cast on 1 st using the backwards loop method. Pm and join for working in the round. [166 (186, 210, 230, 254) (270, 294, 314, 334, 354) sts]

**Round 1:** K1tbl, (p1tbl, k1tbl) twice, k until 6 sts before side stm, (k1tbl, p1tbl) 3 times, sm, k1tbl, (p1tbl, k1tbl) twice, k until 6 sts before BOR, (k1tbl, p1tbl) 3 times.

Repeat last round until body measures 6 (6.25, 6.5, 6.75, 7) (7.25, 7.5, 7.75, 8, 8.25)" / 15 (16, 17, 17, 18) (18, 19, 20, 20, 21) cm from the the point where the front and back pieces are joined, or until desired length.

> **TIP:** *Use a piece of spare yarn as a mock strap to see what your preferred strap length is.*

Switch to US 4 (3.5 mm) needles.

**Next round**: K all sts, removing the side stm along the way.

Using a tapestry needle, insert a scrap piece of yarn in the contrasting color in the round you just knit. This piece of yarn will serve as your lifeline and mark the round to which you will be seaming your edge in order to complete the hem.

**Next 4 rounds:** K all sts.

**Next round (turning round):** P all sts.

**Next 4 rounds:** K all sts.

Bind off loosely, leaving a tail 2x the length of the hem. Fold the hem inwards and whip stitch the bind off edge to the round indicated by the lifeline. Remove lifeline.

## STRAP

At this point, it is recommended to take a piece of spare yarn and insert it through the hems to see what your desired length of the strap is.

Using US 4 (3.5 mm) straight or double pointed needles, cast on 2 sts using the longtail cast on method.

**Next row:** K2. Slide sts to end of needle (or transfer back to left needle).

Repeat last row until tie measures 55 inches (140 cm), or desired length. Bind off and weave in ends. Secure a safety pin to one end of your cord and feed it into the back left, front and back right hems.

## FINISHING

Weave in any loose ends and block the garment using your preferred method.

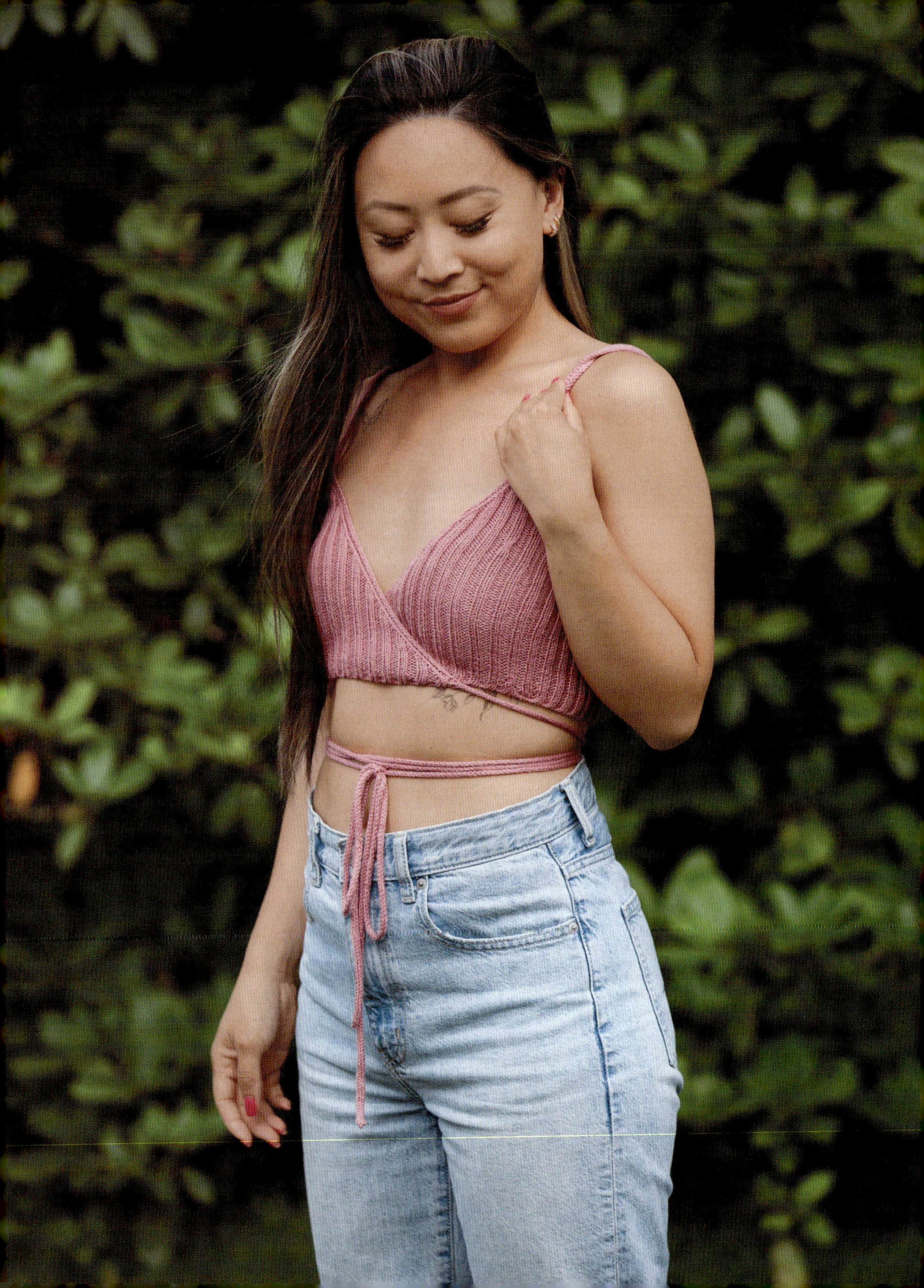

# Camellia Wrap Top

Wrap top, but make it cropped! Part camisole and part ballerina top, the Camellia Wrap Top is a lightweight wrap top that is flattering for all figures. Knit in an all-around ribbing, this repetitive pattern is the perfect recipe for TV knitting, and the result is a stretchy fabric that will hug all your curves. The I-cord ties draw the eyes down to the waist to emphasize your natural shape. Whether you prefer it wrapped once, twice, or three times around your body, the ties allow you to wear the top in your preferred level of snugness. The plunging neckline allows you to show off your favorite necklace, or you can opt to wear a bandeau underneath for more modest coverage. The Camellia Wrap Top will fly off your needles in no time!

## Construction Notes

*The top is worked flat from the bottom up, beginning with a tubular cast on to create a clean, rolled edge. Circular needles are recommended to accommodate for the large number of stitches. Decreases are worked on both ends of the piece to create the deep V-neckline. Once the length of the body is established, stitches are bound off using the tubular bind off method to create the back.*

*The front right piece is continued in pattern, with decreases worked on both sides to create a triangular cup. The remaining cup stitches are worked in double stockinette to create the strap, which is later seamed to the back. The same is repeated for the left front piece and strap. Finally, stitches are picked up from the bottom edge corners of both sides and two I-cords are worked until desired length is achieved for wrapping around your waist.*

## SKILL LEVEL
*Advanced Beginner*

## SIZING
XS (S, M, L, XL) (2XL, 3XL, 4XL, 5XL, 6XL)

29.25 (33, 37.25, 41, 45.25) (49, 53.25, 57, 60.5, 65)" / 74 (84, 95, 104, 115) (124, 135, 145, 154, 165) cm, blocked

## Materials

### Yarn
*Fingering weight, Rowan Summerlite 4ply in color 426 (100% cotton), 191 yds (175 m) per 50-g skein*

*Any fingering weight yarn can be used for this pattern as long as it matches gauge.*

### Yardage/Meterage
270 (345, 395, 495, 600) (650, 730, 825, 910, 1050) yds / 245 (315, 360, 450, 550) (595, 665, 755, 830, 960) m of fingering weight yarn

### Needles
**For body:** *US 2 (2.75 mm) straight or circular needles (two pairs)*

**For straps:** *US 2 (2.75 mm) straight or double pointed needles*

### Notions
*Hook-and-eye closure (optional)*

*Removable stitch markers*

*Scrap yarn for casting on*

*Scrap yarn or stitch holder*

*Sewing needle and matching thread (optional)*

*Stitch markers*

*Tapestry needle*

## GAUGE

28 sts x 36 rows = 4 inches (10 cm) in 2x2 ribbing worked flat (blocked and stretched)

**NOTE:** *It is difficult to measure gauge accurately when it comes to ribbing due to the amount of stretch. If you are able to get close to gauge stretched OR unstretched, the garment will fit.*

## TECHNIQUES

2x2 Tubular Cast On *(instructions within pattern)*
Double Stockinette Stitch *(page 153)*
I-Cord *(page 153)*
Kitchener Stitch *(page 147)*
Provisional Cast On *(page 145)*
Tubular Bind Off *(instructions within pattern)*
Horizontal Invisible Seaming *(page 149)*

## ABBREVIATIONS

| | |
|---|---|
| 2x2 ribbing | *k2, p2; repeat from * until end |
| dec | decrease |
| k | knit |
| k2tog | knit 2 sts together [1 st decreased] |
| p | purl |
| p2tog | purl 2 sts together [1 st decreased] |
| patt | pattern |
| rem | remain(ing) |
| rep | repeat |
| RS | right side |
| sl1wyib | slip 1 st purlwise with yarn in back |
| sl2wyib | slip 2 sts purlwise with yarn in back |
| sl1wyif | slip 1 st purlwise with yarn in front |
| sl2wyif | slip 2 sts purlwise with yarn in front |
| ssk | slip 2 sts knitwise, one at a time; move both stitches back to the left needle; knit these 2 sts together through the back loops [1 st decreased] |
| st(s) | stitch(es) |
| stm | stitch marker |
| WS | wrong side |

## SIZING CHART

|  | XS | S | M | L | XL | 2XL | 3XL | 4XL | 5XL | 6XL |  |
|---|---|---|---|---|---|---|---|---|---|---|---|
| A) Body Circumference (Tied) | 29.25 | 33 | 37.25 | 41 | 45.25 | 49 | 53.25 | 57 | 60.5 | 65 | in |
|  | 74 | 84 | 95 | 104 | 115 | 124 | 135 | 145 | 154 | 165 | cm |
| B) V-Neck Depth* | 4.75 | 5.5 | 6.25 | 7.25 | 7.5 | 8.75 | 9 | 10.25 | 10.25 | 11.75 | in |
|  | 12 | 14 | 16 | 19 | 19 | 23 | 23 | 26 | 26 | 30 | cm |
| C) Front Armhole Depth | 2.75 | 3.25 | 4 | 4.5 | 5 | 6 | 6.5 | 6.75 | 7.25 | 8.25 | in |
|  | 7 | 9 | 10 | 12 | 13 | 15 | 16 | 17 | 19 | 21 | cm |
| D) Length to Armhole | 5.75 | 6.75 | 6.75 | 8 | 8 | 9 | 9 | 10.25 | 10.25 | 11.25 | in |
|  | 14 | 17 | 17 | 20 | 20 | 23 | 23 | 26 | 26 | 29 | cm |

The top is designed with -1.5 to 1.5 inches (-4 to 4 cm) of negative to positive ease. Sample shown is knit in size XS. If in between sizes, it is recommended to select the smaller size.

*The V-neck depth is dependent on how tightly the top is wrapped around your body, which affects the amount of fabric pulled towards the back. If wrapped more loosely, the depth will increase. If wrapped more tightly, the depth will decrease.

## SCHEMATIC

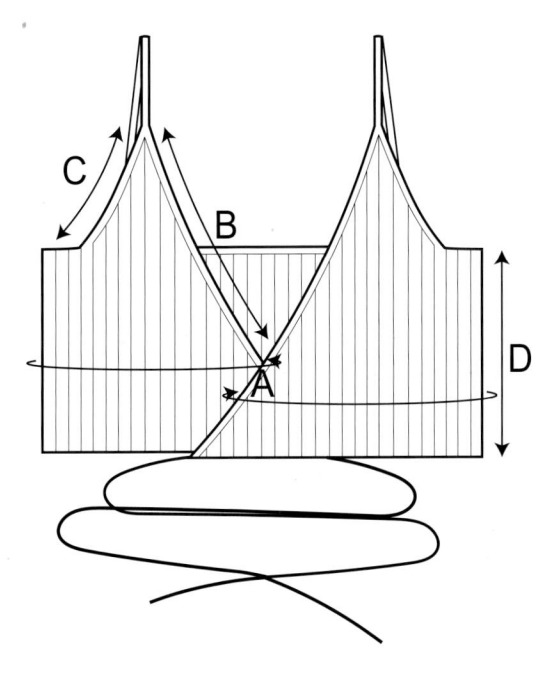

# CAMELLIA WRAP TOP PATTERN

## BODY
### 2x2 Tubular Cast On

Using US 2 (2.75 mm) needles and scrap yarn, cast on 119 (135, 149, 165, 181) (197, 213, 227, 243, 259) sts using the provisional cast on method.

Join working yarn at the slipknot end of the provisional cast on. Beginning with a knit row, work 4 rows of stockinette stitch.

Remove the provisional cast on and slip those live sts on to another needle. Line up those needles and create a fold so the purl sts are facing each other.

**Set-up row 1 (RS):** *K2 from the front needle, p2 from the back needle; rep from * until last 2 sts *(1 st on each needle)*, k1 from the front needle and k1 from the back needle. [238 (270, 298, 330, 362) (394, 426, 454, 486, 518) sts]

**Set-up row 2 (WS):** *P2, k2; rep from * until last 2 sts, p2.

**Set-up row 3:** *K2, p2; rep from * until last 2 sts, k2.

**Set-up row 4:** Repeat set-up row 2.

> **TIP:** *Use a removable stitch marker to mark the RS of your garment, as it can be easy to confuse the sides as you progress with the project!*

### Begin Decreases

**Row 1 (RS, dec):** Sl1wyib, k1, p2, ssk, (p2, k2) until last 8 sts, p2, k2tog, p2, k2. [236 (268, 296, 328, 360) (392, 424, 452, 484, 516) sts rem, 2 sts decreased]

**Row 2 (WS):** Sl1wyif, p1, k2, p1, (k2, p2) until last 7 sts, k2, p1, k2, p2.

**Row 3 (dec):** Sl1wyib, k1, p2, ssk, p1, (k2, p2) until last 9 sts, k2, p1, k2tog, p2, k2. [234 (266, 294, 326, 358) (390, 422, 450, 482, 514) sts rem, 2 sts decreased]

**Row 4:** Sl1wyif, p1, k2, p1, k1, (p2, k2) until last 8 sts, p2, k1, p1, k2, p2.

**Row 5 (dec):** Sl1wyib, k1, p2, ssk, (k2, p2) until last 8 sts, k2, k2tog, p2, k2. [232 (264, 292, 324, 356) (388, 420, 448, 480, 512) sts rem, 2 sts decreased]

**Row 6:** Sl1wyif, p1, k2, p3, (k2, p2) until last 9 sts, k2, p3, k2, p2.

**Row 7 (dec):** Sl1wyib, k1, p2, ssk, k1, (p2, k2) until last 9 sts, p2, k1, k2tog, p2, k2. [230 (262, 290, 322, 354) (386, 418, 446, 478, 510) sts rem, 2 sts decreased]

**Row 8:** Sl1wyif, p1, (k2, p2) until end.

Repeat rows 1–8 a total of 4 (5, 5, 6, 6) (7, 7, 8, 8, 9) more times until 198 (222, 250, 274, 306) (330, 362, 382, 414, 438) sts rem.

Repeat rows 1–6 a total of 1 more time until 192 (216, 244, 268, 300) (324, 356, 376, 408, 432) sts rem.

### Prepare for Tubular Bind Off

You will now be binding off sts for the back piece only. After binding off the center sts, you will have live sts on both sides of the bind off that make up the front pieces.

**Next row (RS):** Sl1wyib, k1, p2, ssk, work in patt for 34 (38, 42, 50, 54) (62, 66, 70, 74, 82) sts. Place marker. Sl1wyif, (k2, sl2wyif) 27 (31, 36, 38, 44) (46, 52, 55, 61, 63) times, k2, sl1wyif. Place marker. Work in patt for 34 (38, 42, 50, 54) (62, 66, 70, 74, 82) sts, k2tog, p2, k2.

**Next row (WS):** Sl1wyif, work in patt until stm. Remove marker and place the 39 (43, 47, 55, 59) (67, 71, 75, 79, 87) sts you just worked for the Front Left on a holder or spare yarn to return to later. K1, (sl2wyif, k2) until 3 sts before stm, sl2wyif, k1. Remove marker and place rem 39 (43, 47, 55, 59) (67, 71, 75, 79, 87) for the Front Right on a holder or spare yarn to return to later. Break yarn, leaving a tail approximately 3x the length of the back sts for bind off.

You will now be rearranging your back sts so that all the knit sts will be slipped to one needle, and all the purl sts will be slipped to another needle and sit at the back. Ensure you have an equal number of sts on each needle. Bind off using Kitchener stitch.

## FRONT RIGHT

Return sts to needle with the WS facing you. Pick up 1 st from the back bind off and move to the left-hand needle. [40 (44, 48, 56, 60) (68, 72, 76, 80, 88) sts]

**Next row (WS):** Bind off 2 sts, work rem sts in patt. [38 (42, 46, 54, 58) (66, 70, 74, 78, 86) sts rem, 2 sts decreased]

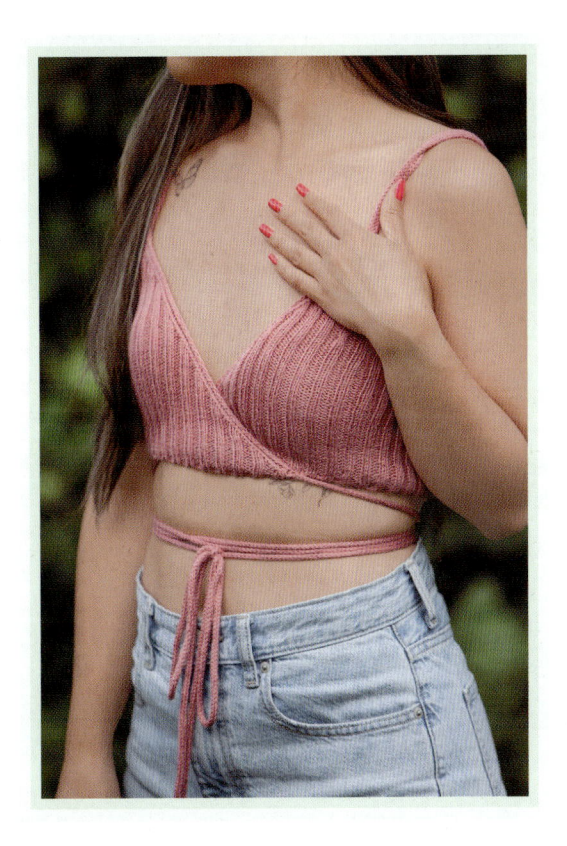

### Begin Decreases

**Next row (RS, dec):** Sl1wyib, k1, p2, ssk, work in patt until last 6 sts, k2tog, p2, k2. [36 (40, 44, 52, 56) (64, 68, 72, 76, 84) sts rem, 2 sts decreased]

**Next row (WS):** Sl1wyif, work rem sts in patt.

Repeat last 2 rows a total of 12 (14, 16, 20, 22) (26, 28, 30, 32, 36) more times until 12 sts rem.

**Row 1 (RS, dec):** Sl1wyib, k1, p2, ssk, k2tog, p2, k2. [10 sts rem, 2 sts decreased]

**Row 2 (WS):** Sl1wyif, p1, (k2, p2) twice.

**Row 3:** Sl1wyib, k1, p2tog, k2tog, p2tog, k2. [7 sts rem, 3 sts decreased]

**Row 4:** Sl2wyif, k1, sl1wyif, k1, sl2wyif.

**Row 5:** K2, sl1wyif, k1, sl1wyif, k2.

Repeat rows 4–5 until strap measures 11 (11.25, 11.5, 11.75, 12) (12.25, 12.5, 12.75, 13, 13.25)" / 28 (29, 29, 30, 30) (31, 32, 32, 33, 34) cm. These are the suggested lengths for regular straps (unstretched). For cross back straps, you will need to add approximately 4–5 inches (10–13 cm) of length. Bind off and leave a 4-inch (10-cm) tail for seaming.

## FRONT LEFT

Return sts to needle with the RS facing you. Pick up 1 st from the back bind off and move to the left-hand needle. [40 (44, 48, 56, 60) (68, 72, 76, 80, 88) sts]

**Next row (RS):** Bind off 2 sts, k2, p2, ssk, work in patt until last 6 sts, k2tog, p2, k2. [36 (40, 44, 52, 56) (64, 68, 72, 76, 84) sts rem, 4 sts decreased]

### Continue Decreases

**Next row (WS):** Sl1wyif, work rem sts in patt.

**Next row (RS, dec):** Sl1wyib, k1, p2, ssk, work in patt until last 6 sts, k2tog, p2, k2 [34 (38, 42, 50, 54) (62, 66, 70, 74, 82) sts rem, 2 sts decreased]

Repeat last 2 rows a total of 11 (13, 15, 19, 21) (25, 27, 29, 31, 35) more times until 12 sts rem. Work one more WS row.

**Row 1 (RS, dec):** Sl1wyib, k1, p2, ssk, k2tog, p2, k2. [10 sts rem, 2 sts decreased]

**Row 2 (WS):** Sl1wyif, p1, (k2, p2) twice.

**Row 3:** Sl1wyib, k1, p2tog, k2tog, p2tog, k2. [7 sts rem, 3 sts decreased]

**Row 4:** Sl2wyif, k1, sl1wyif, k1, sl2wyif.

**Row 5:** K2, sl1wyif, k1, sl1wyif, k2.

Repeat rows 4–5 until strap measures 11 (11.25, 11.5, 11.75, 12) (12.25, 12.5, 12.75, 13, 13.25)" / 28 (29, 29, 30, 30) (31, 32, 32, 33, 34) cm or until desired length to match the front right strap. Bind off and leave a 4-inch (10-cm) tail for seaming.

## FRONT RIGHT TIE

With the RS facing and beginning at the bottom edge corner, use US 2 (2.75 mm) straight or double pointed needles to pick up and k4. Slide sts to end of needle (or transfer back to left needle). Do not turn.

**Next row:** K4, slide sts to end of needle (or transfer back to left needle).

Repeat last row until I-cord measures 60 (65, 75, 80, 90) (95, 100, 105, 110, 115)" / 153 (166, 191, 204, 229) (242, 254, 267, 280, 293) cm, or until your desired length. The suggested length will roughly wrap around your waist a total of 3 times.

## FRONT LEFT TIE

With the RS facing and beginning at 4 sts from the bottom edge corner, use US 2 (2.75 mm) straight or double pointed needles to pick up and k4. Slide sts to end of needle (or transfer back to left needle). Do not turn.

**Next row:** K4, slide sts to end of needle (or transfer back to left needle).

Repeat last row until I-cord measures 60 (65, 75, 80, 90) (95, 100, 105, 110, 115)" / 153 (166, 191, 204, 229) (242, 254, 267, 280, 293) cm or until your desired length to match the front right tie.

## FINISHING

Weave in any loose ends. Block your project using your preferred method. I recommend seaming the straps after blocking, so you can better visualize placement.

Lay your top flat with the front pieces folded over with an overlap in the front (see Schematic image, page 137). Using removable stms, mark where the ends of the straps are to be seamed on the body. For regular straps, a good place to start would be on the center back side of the front pieces. However, everyone's body is different and you may need to adjust accordingly. Feel free to use safety pins to test out placement. Once placement is decided, use the horizontal invisible seaming technique to seam the strap to the body.

For additional security, you can use a sewing needle and thread to attach a hook-and-eye closure on the WS of the front pieces. To find the ideal placement for the closure, try on the garment and mark the point in which the front pieces meet at the V-neck and are no longer overlapping.

# Techniques

In this section, you will find tutorials on how to approach some of the most common techniques used in this book. While these are my go-to methods, there are often multiple ways to achieve the same outcome. Feel free to defer to your personal preference!

## CASTING ON
### Backwards Loop Cast On

The backwards loop cast on is one of the simplest cast on methods for a quick and stretchy fabric edge. It is a good method to use when casting on mid-row or round or at the end of a row or round.

**Step 1:** Make a slipknot on the right needle. If casting on in an existing project, this step is not necessary.

**Step 2:** Wind the working yarn around your left thumb in a counterclockwise motion.

**Step 3:** Insert the right needle into the loop through the base of your thumb and over the yarn at the top of your thumb.

**Step 4:** Tighten the stitch by pulling on the working yarn.

Repeat steps 2–4 until all the stitches are cast on.

## I-Cord Cast On

The I-cord cast on creates a clean, rounded edge at the beginning of a project.

**Step 1:** Cast on 3 stitches using your preferred method.

**Step 2:** Slip the 3 stitches over to your left needle. Do not turn your work. The working yarn should be coming from the last stitch rather than the first stitch.

**Step 3:** Pull the working yarn across the back of the cast on stitches. Knit 2 stitches. Knit through the front *and* back of the third stitch. You should have a total of 4 stitches on your right needle.

**Step 4:** Slip all 4 stitches from your right needle to your left needle.

Repeat steps 3 and 4 until all the stitches are cast on, plus 3 additional stitches for finishing (for example, if your pattern calls for you to cast on 164 stitches, ensure you have 167 stitches before you move forward with the pattern). With each repeat, 1 stitch is added to your left needle. Once completed, slip the 4 stitches from your right needle to your left needle. K2tog twice. Slip the 2 stitches back to the left needle, then k2tog.

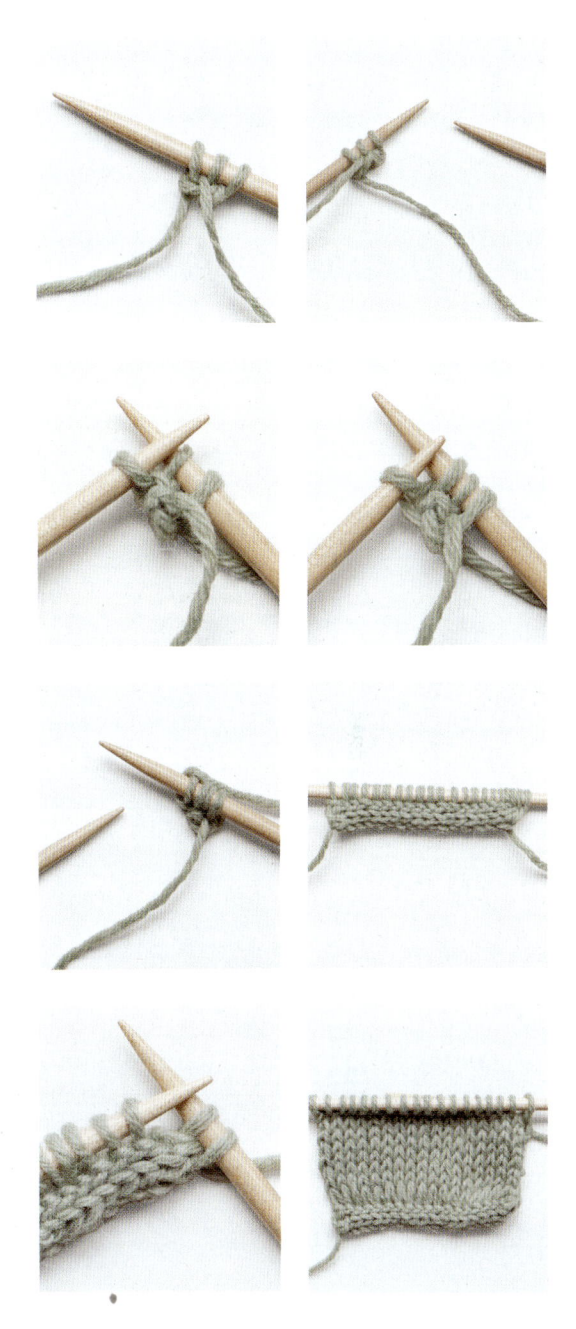

## Longtail Cast On

The longtail cast on method is one of the most frequently used methods. It creates a firm yet elastic edge.

**Step 1:** Make a slipknot on the right needle. Wind the tail around your left thumb. Wrap the working yarn over your left index finger. Secure the ends in your palm for leverage.

**Step 2:** Insert the right needle upwards in the loop on your thumb. With the same needle, draw the working yarn through the loop to form a stitch.

**Step 3:** Take your thumb out of the loop and tighten the loop on the needle. Rewrap the tail around your left thumb.

Repeat steps 2 and 3 until all the stitches are cast on.

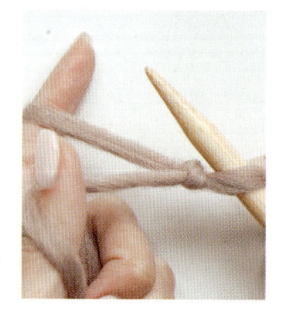

## Provisional Cast On (Crochet Chain Method)

A provisional cast on temporarily holds onto live stitches to be returned to later. There are multiple approaches to this technique. This book will explore the crochet method using a locking stitch marker and a crochet hook the same size or slightly larger than your intended knitting needle. Feel free to use your preferred method for the patterns in this book.

With the crochet method, you will pick up and knit stitches into the back of a crochet chain with the working yarn, resulting in a completed row of stitches. Once the pattern calls for you to remove the provisional cast on, you will simply remove the locking stitch marker and pull on the tail end of the crochet chain, releasing the live stitches.

Before you begin, refer to your pattern for the number of cast on stitches required. It is recommended to chain additional stitches so you don't accidentally miss one (for example, if the pattern calls for casting on 40 stitches, chain 45 stitches).

**Step 1:** Using contrasting waste yarn, make a slipknot and place it on the crochet hook. Create a crochet chain that is several stitches longer than the number of cast on stitches required for the pattern. When completed, remove the hook and clip the locking stitch marker into the final chain to keep the chain from unraveling. Break the waste yarn.

**Step 2:** Use your project yarn and needle to knit into the back of this crochet chain. Continue until the remainder of your stitches are cast on.

Continue with the pattern as instructed. Once you are ready to use these live stitches, remove the locking stitch marker. Gently pull on that end of the contrasting yarn and move the live stitches over one by one to your working needle until all the stitches are on your needle.

# BINDING OFF
## 3-Needle Bind Off

This bind off is used to join two edges that have the same number of stitches. This is most commonly used to join live shoulder edges that have been placed on holders. You will need three needles for this technique, hence the name.

**Step 1:** Flip your work inside out so the right sides of the two pieces are facing each other and the needles are parallel.

**Step 2:** Insert a third needle knitwise into the first stitch of each needle and wrap the yarn around the needle as if to knit. Knit these 2 stitches together and slip them off the needle.

**Step 3:** Knit the next 2 stitches together in the same way as shown.

**Step 4:** Slip the first stitch on the third needle over the second stitch and off the needle.

Repeat steps 3 and 4 until all the stitches are bound off.

## Kitchener Stitch

This technique is used to graft two pieces of live stitches together. Position your work so the wrong sides of the two pieces are facing each other and the needles are parallel.

**Step 1:** Insert your tapestry needle purlwise through the first stitch on the front needle. Pull the yarn through, leaving that stitch on the knitting needle.

**Step 2:** Insert your tapestry needle knitwise through the first stitch on the back needle. Pull the yarn though, leaving the stitch on the knitting needle.

**Step 3:** Insert your tapestry needle knitwise through the first stitch on the front needle, slip the stitch off the needle, and insert the tapestry needle purlwise through the next stitch on the front needle. Pull the yarn through, leaving this stitch on the needle.

**Step 4:** Insert your tapestry needle purlwise through the first stitch on the back needle. Slip the stitch off the needle and insert the tapestry needle knitwise through the next stitch on the back needle. Pull the yarn through, leaving this stitch on the needle.

Repeat steps 3 and 4 on each stitch until all stitches on both the front and back needles have been grafted. Fasten off and weave in the ends.

Techniques

147

## I-Cord Bind Off

An I-cord bind off creates a beautiful, rounded edge for your pattern. It can be worked on either the RS or WS of the work depending on the pattern.

**Step 1:** Using your right needle, insert it between the first and second stitch of your left needle. Wrap the working yarn around your right needle and draw it up so you have a new stitch. Place the new stitch onto the left needle.

**Step 2:** Repeat one more time so you have a total of 2 new stitches.

**Step 3:** K1, ssk from the left needle. Move the 2 stitches back to the left needle.

Repeat the last step until no stitches remain. Bind off. If working in the round, the pattern may call for you to seam the ends of the I-cord together. If so, leave a tail long enough to weave in any ends, so there are no gaps from the beginning and end of the I-cord bind off.

# SEAMING
## Horizontal Invisible Seam

This seaming technique is used to join two bound-off edges, most commonly for shoulder seams. In order to work this seam, you will need a tapestry needle and yarn. The recommended amount of yarn is approximately 3 times the length of the edge.

**Step 1:** Position your work so that the bound-off edges are together and lined up stitch for stitch. Thread your tapestry needle with your working yarn.

**Step 2:** Insert your tapestry needle under and out through the center of the first V stitch of one piece. Pull the yarn through.

**Step 3:** Insert your tapestry needle under the corresponding V stitch on the other piece and pull the yarn through.

Repeat steps 2 and 3 until the seam is complete.

Techniques       149

## Mattress Stitch

This seaming technique is used to join two edges and is most commonly used for side seams. In order to work this seam, you will need a tapestry needle and yarn. The recommended amount of yarn is approximately 3 times the length of the edge.

**Step 1:** Position your work so that the right side is facing you, and the edges are lined up side by side. Thread your tapestry needle with your working yarn.

**Step 2:** Insert your tapestry needle under the first edge running stitch of one piece, the bar between the Vs, and pull the yarn through.

**Step 3:** Insert your tapestry needle under the corresponding running stitch on the other piece and pull the yarn through. Gently pull on your working yarn to bring the seams neatly together. Avoid pulling too hard as that will result in bunching of the fabric.

Repeat steps 2 and 3 until the seam is complete.

## Whip Stitch

This seaming technique is used to join two edges together. It is not an invisible seam, so it is typically used in folded hems where the edge is hidden.

**Step 1:** Line up the edges of the pieces to be seamed together. Thread your tapestry needle with your working yarn.

**Step 2:** Insert your tapestry needle from back to front along the edge of the right side of both pieces. Insert the needle from back to front through the next edge stitch. Pull the yarn through, allowing the yarn to wrap over the top edge.

Repeat the last step until the seam is complete.

# SHORT ROW SHAPING
## German Short Rows

Short rows are a technique used to work extra rows across a portion of the stitches on the needles, lengthening the fabric of a specific area where the short rows are worked. Short rows are commonly used to shape shoulders and lengthen the back piece of a garment, raising the fabric at the back neck. German short rows are a technique used for short row shaping with minimal gaps or distorted stitches.

**Step 1:** With the right side facing you, work the number of stitches called for in the pattern. Turn work.

**Step 2:** With the yarn in front, slip the first stitch purlwise. Tug the yarn up and over the needle. This makes a "double" stitch (MDS). Continue working the row as instructed in pattern. Turn work.

**Step 3:** Slip the next stitch purlwise with the yarn in front. Tug the yarn up and over the needle. This makes another MDS. Continue row as instructed in pattern.

**Step 4:** Continue following the pattern as instructed. When you reach a double stitch (DS), you work the DS as if it were 1 stitch (either knitting 2 stitches together or purling 2 stitches together depending on the side of the work you are on).

# OTHER TECHNIQUES
## Creating a Fringe

Adding a fringe is a fun and easy way to add a decorative element to any project. This technique uses simple tools you likely already have in your arsenal: a pair of scissors, yarn and a crochet hook.

**Step 1:** Determine the length and amount of fringe you want to create for your project. Because the yarn will need to be folded in half, you will require double the length of yarn for your desired length of fringe. For example, if you want a 5-inch (13-cm) fringe, you will need to cut a 10-inch (25-cm) piece of yarn per desired fringe.

**Step 2:** Insert your crochet hook into the edge stitch. Take one piece of yarn, fold it in half and secure it onto the hook. Pull the length of yarn through the loop, approximately an inch (2.5 cm) below the stitch.

**Step 3:** Using your other hand, take the two ends of the yarn and feed it into the loop you just created. Pull the ends tightly to secure the fringe.

Repeat steps 2 and 3 until all the fringe pieces are secured. Use scissors to trim the ends to create a cleaner edge.

Light & Breezy Knitwear

## Double Stockinette Stitch

The double stockinette stitch is a popular stitch because it has the same look as the classic stockinette stitch but is also reversible and won't cause your fabric to curl. While time consuming to knit, the result is a thick and squishy fabric that is highly versatile.

**Step 1:** Cast on the number of stitches required for the pattern.

**Step 2:** Knit the first stitch.

**Step 3:** Slip the next stitch purlwise with yarn in front.

**Step 4:** Repeat steps 2 and 3 until the end of the row. Turn your work.

Repeat steps 2–4 until the desired length of the fabric is achieved. Bind off all stitches.

## I-Cord

I-cords are knit tubes of fabric and commonly used for components like ties and drawstrings. To create an I-cord, you will need either circular needles or double pointed needles. The latter is my preference, because the needles are shorter and therefore easier to slide your stitches from one end to the other.

**Step 1:** Cast on the number of stitches required for the pattern. Slide these stitches to the right end of the left needle.

**Step 2:** Knit across all stitches.

**Step 3:** Slide these stitches to the right end of the left needle.

Repeat steps 2 and 3 until the desired length of the I-cord is achieved. Bind off all stitches.

Techniques

# Resources

The following list includes useful links that every knitter or designer should have handy. For example, the Craft Yarn Council has entire sections of their website dedicated to standards and guidelines related to yarn weight, garment measurements, tool sizes and more. The list also includes other popular resources you can use to improve your techniques, browse for yarn or find me on the web.

**Craft Yarn Council:** craftyarncouncil.com

**Ravelry:** ravelry.com

**Techniques:** *Vogue® Knitting, The Ultimate Knitting Book*

**YarnSub:** yarnsub.com

**My Website:** knitwearbyjoan.com

**Knitwear by Joan Patterns (Ravelry):** ravelry.com/designers/joan-ho

**Knitwear by Joan Patterns (Etsy):** etsy.com/shop/knitwearbyjoan

# Acknowledgments

### To Jacky
Thank you for not telling me I'm crazy for writing two books in two years! Or at least, thanks for not saying it out loud. Thanks for believing in me from the very beginning and for giving me the confidence to pursue this little dream of mine. Your faith in me keeps me going on the toughest of days. I love you!

### To My Family
Mom and Dad, thank you for teaching me early on in life that hard work pays off. In leading by example, you have shown me that most challenges in life are temporary and toughness builds character. There have been many instances where it's been easy to give up, but the values you've instilled in me have propelled me to move forward one foot at a time. Jocelyn, thanks for being my sounding board for everything, both craft and non-craft related. Joey, thanks for reminding me what is truly important in life.

### To My Friends
It looks like I'll be taking over your social media feeds once again with this book! Jokes aside, your encouragement and unwavering support gave me the motivation to see this project through. Christie, what can I say? You've been my number one cheerleader since we were thirteen, and I truly don't know what I'd do without you. Thanks for always giving me your 125%—that extra 25% has gotten me through particularly rough days where I lacked confidence in my own abilities. Loretta, your optimism, steadfastness and calm demeanor are all traits that I admire about you and have relied on throughout our 20+ years of friendship. I know I can always count on you, and that's all a girl can ever ask for.

### To Sarah
Thank you so much for all the hard work you've put into making my second book a reality. Your attention to detail, patience and flexibility has been integral to this creative journey of mine. It's been an honor to work with you for a second time!

### To Page Street Publishing
Thank you so much for your support in continuing to make my dreams come true. The past couple of years spent working on these two books have been some of the most fulfilling times of my life, and it all started because you believed in my vision. I will forever be grateful for the opportunities you've given me. Thank you to everyone on the Page Street Publishing team for your guidance and expertise throughout this entire process!

*(continued)*

### To My Testers

Thank you for being the most amazing group of test knitters a girl can only dream of working with! I wouldn't be able to do this without your hard work and feedback. Your enthusiasm and support help me become a better designer every day, and I can't thank you enough for it.

### To My Suppliers

Thank you to the following companies for sending me their beautiful yarns to create the designs in this book. Your generosity is greatly appreciated!

**Koigu Wool Designs**
koigu.com

**Summer Camp Fibers**
summercampfibers.com

# About the Author

Joan Ho is an independent knitwear designer specializing in garments and accessories. She is the author of *Cable Knit Style* as well as the former co-owner of HANK & HOOK, which brought popular European yarn brands and DIY kits to a North American audience. During this time, she delved into pattern writing and fell in love with the creative aspect of design. She has since published knitting patterns both independently and as a freelance designer.

Joan lives in Mississauga, Ontario, with her husband, Jacky, and their two cats, Tiger and Linden. When not knitting, she is probably reading romantasy, crafting or at the theater. *Light & Breezy Knitwear* is her second book.

Her website is knitwearbyjoan.com.

# Index

## A
abbreviations, 22, 30, 36, 46, 55, 67, 76, 86, 92, 99, 108, 114, 122, 128, 136
advanced patterns, 9
armhole depth, 10
armhole edge, 52, 80–81
athleisure. See loungewear

## B
backwards loop cast on, 142
beginner patterns, 9
binding off, 146–148
    3-needle, 146
    I-cord, 148
    Kitchener stitch, 147
blocking, 15–16
body circumference, 10
bottoms
    Ivy Mesh Skirt, 97–105
    Poppy Pocket Shorts, 65–73
    Sakura Skirt, 29–33
bralettes
    Dahlia Bralette, 85–89
    Ivy Mesh Bralette, 91–96
buttons, snap-on, 14, 64

## C
Camellia Wrap Top, 135–141
casting on, 142–145
    backwards loop, 142
    I-cord, 143
    longtail, 144
    provisional, 145

circular needles, 13
coverups
    Ivy Mesh Bralette, 91–96
    Ivy Mesh Skirt, 97–105
crochet chain method, 145

## D
Dahlia Bralette, 85–89
difficulty levels, 9
double pointed needles (DPNs), 13
double stockinette stitch, 153

## E
ease, 10
elastic, 14, 26, 33

## F
fasteners, 14
fit, 9–10
fringe, 105, 152

## G
garment length, 10
gauge, 11–12, 19, 75, 121, 136
gauge swatch, 11–12
German short rows, 151

## H
halter top, Plume Halter, 121–125
handknits
    caring for, 15–17
    storage of, 17
handwashing, 16–17
hems
    folded, 24, 26, 32, 40, 48, 57, 69, 101
    top, 32, 69, 101, 130–132
    underbust, 39–40

Hibiscus Top, 127–133
Hollyberry Tee, 113–117
horizontal invisible seam, 149

## I
I-cord bind off, 24, 33, 148
I-cord cast on, 143
I-cord drawstring, 73, 102
I-cord knitting, 13
I-cords, 153
intermediate patterns, 9
Iris Racerback Tank, 45–52
Ivy Mesh Bralette, 91–96
Ivy Mesh Skirt, 97–105

## K
Kitchener stitch, 147
knitting charts, 12–13
knitwear
    caring for, 15–17
    storage of, 17

## L
lacework, 19, 83
longtail cast on, 144
loungewear, 43–81
    Iris Racerback Tank, 45–52
    Poppy Pocket Shorts, 65–73
    Poppy Pocket Tee, 53–64
    Wisteria Tank, 75–81

## M
Mariposa Top, 107–111
mattress stitch, 150
measurements, 9–10

## N
natural fibers, 16
neckband, 52, 62

neck bind off, 58
necklines, 50, 81
needles, 13, 14, 15
   circular, 13
   double pointed, 13
   sewing, 14
   straight, 13
   tapestry, 15
negative ease, 10
neutral ease, 10
notions, 14–15

## P

patterns, difficulty levels, 9
Petunia Top, 35–41
Plume Halter, 121–125
pockets, 57–59, 62–64, 71–73
Poppy Pocket Shorts, 65–73
Poppy Pocket Tee, 53–64
positive ease, 10
provisional cast on, 145

## R

Ravelry, 11, 154
removable stitch markers, 15
resources, 154

## S

Sakura Skirt, 29–33
Sakura Top, 21–27
schematics, 9
seams
   horizontal invisible, 149
   mattress stitch, 150
   pocket, 71
   shoulder, 62, 80, 116
   side, 117
   whip stitch, 150

sewing needles, 14
short row shaping, 151
shorts, Poppy Pocket Shorts, 65–73
shoulder seams, 62, 80, 116
shoulder straps, 89, 111
side seams, 117
sizing chart
   Camellia Wrap Top, 137
   Dahlia Bralette, 87
   Hibiscus Top, 129
   Hollyberry Tee, 115
   Iris Racerback Tank, 47
   Ivy Mesh Bralette, 93
   Ivy Mesh Skirt, 100
   Mariposa Top, 109
   Petunia Top, 37
   Plume Halter, 123
   Poppy Pocket Shorts, 68
   Poppy Pocket Tee, 56
   Sakura Skirt, 31
   Sakura Top, 23
   Wisteria Tank, 77
sizing table, 9–10
skirts
   Ivy Mesh Skirt, 97–105
   Sakura Skirt, 29–33
sleeve circumference, 10
sleeve length, 10
sleeves, 62
snap-on buttons, 14, 64, 71, 73
standard stitch markers, 15
steam blocking, 16
stitches
   double stockinette, 153
   Kitchener, 147

mattress, 150
whip, 150
stitch holders, 14
stitch markers, 15
storage, 17
straight needles, 13
straps, 111, 124–125, 133
substitute yarns, 11
superwash wool, 16
swatch, gauge, 11–12
synthetic fibers, 16

## T

tank tops
   Iris Racerback Tank, 45–52
   Wisteria Tank, 75–81
tapestry needles, 15
tassels, 102–105
techniques, 142–153
   3-needle bind off, 146
   backwards loop cast on, 142
   double stockinette stitch, 153
   fringe, 152
   German short rows, 151
   horizontal invisible seam, 149
   I-cord bind off, 148
   I-cord cast on, 143
   I-cords, 153
   Kitchener stitch, 147
   longtail cast on, 144
   mattress stitch, 150
   provisional cast on, 145
   whip stitch, 150
thread, 14

3-needle bind off, 146

tops
- Camellia Wrap Top, 135–141
- Dahlia Bralette, 85–89
- Hibiscus Top, 127–133
- Hollyberry Tee, 113–117
- Iris Racerback Tank, 45–52
- Ivy Mesh Bralette, 91–96
- Mariposa Top, 107–111
- Petunia Top, 35–41
- Plume Halter, 121–125
- Poppy Pocket Tee, 53–64
- Sakura Top, 21–27
- Wisteria Tank, 75–81

t-shirts
- Hollyberry Tee, 113–117
- Poppy Pocket Tee, 53–64

## W

washing, 16–17

wet blocking, 16

whip stitch, 150

Wisteria Tank, 75–81

wrap top, Camellia Wrap Top, 135–141

## Y

yarn, 11–12
- substitutes, 11

YarnSub, 11, 154